I

Gordc er

Patrick Gordon Walker in his Oxford Air Squadron outfit, as a don at Christ Church

Patrick Gordon Walker

A Political and Family History

ALAN GORDON WALKER

UMBRIA PRESS

First published 2022 by Umbria Press
London SW15 5DP
umbriapress.co.uk

Designed by Louise Millar

Printed by Bell & Bain Ltd, Glasgow
bell-bain.com

ISBN 978 1 910074 42 8

IN MEMORIAM

Patrick Gordon Walker 1907–1980

Audrey Gordon Walker 1911–2005

Judith Greene (Gordon Walker) 1936–2016

Ann Gordon-Walker 1944–2021

Robin Gordon-Walker 1946–2016

………………………………………..

And for Caroline Gordon-Walker 1937–

With all love to:

Louise,

Tom and Helen, Emily and Al,

and Maya, Rufus and Max

Contents

Acknowledgements

I have relied on family trees and histories of the family prepared by my late twin brother Robin and there have been many times when I have deeply missed his wisdom and knowledge on the family and his photographic memory. The book would have been richer from his expert advice and input.

For my mother Audrey's family, I have been greatly helped by our cousin Andrew Rudolf, who has provided much information on the Jamaican heritage of my maternal grandparents and of their families. He has been a life-long friend to the Gordon Walker family, and he is a special and deeply religious man. His wife, Juliet, sadly died on 18 March 2018.

I have rare copies of all my father's published books, which I have reread, and have had access to his *Political Diaries*, edited by Robert Pearce and published by the Historians' Press, which has an excellent introduction. The diaries cover the Oxford years (1932–1938), the Second World War (1939–1945), the Labour government of 1945–1951, opposition and the Gaitskell years (1952–1963) and the Wilson years (1963–1971).

An addendum to this book is an edited version of my father's diary account of his wartime visit to Belsen, which first appeared in his book *The Lid Lifts*, published in 1945, when he worked for the BBC German Service. The account is taken from his published diaries, which concentrated on his second visit, and covers the period from 17 to 23 April 1945, including his arrival in Belsen on Friday 20th. His April 1945 'Reflections on Belsen' did not appear in *The Lid Lifts*, for whose publication there were certain changes and omissions. *The Lid Lifts* has been out of print since its first publication, a necessarily limited edition because of the paper and other shortages at the end of the war.

My father's political papers are held in the archives of Churchill College, Cambridge.

Many illustrations are included, all from family collections, passed down through the generations.

Alan Gordon Walker, July 2022

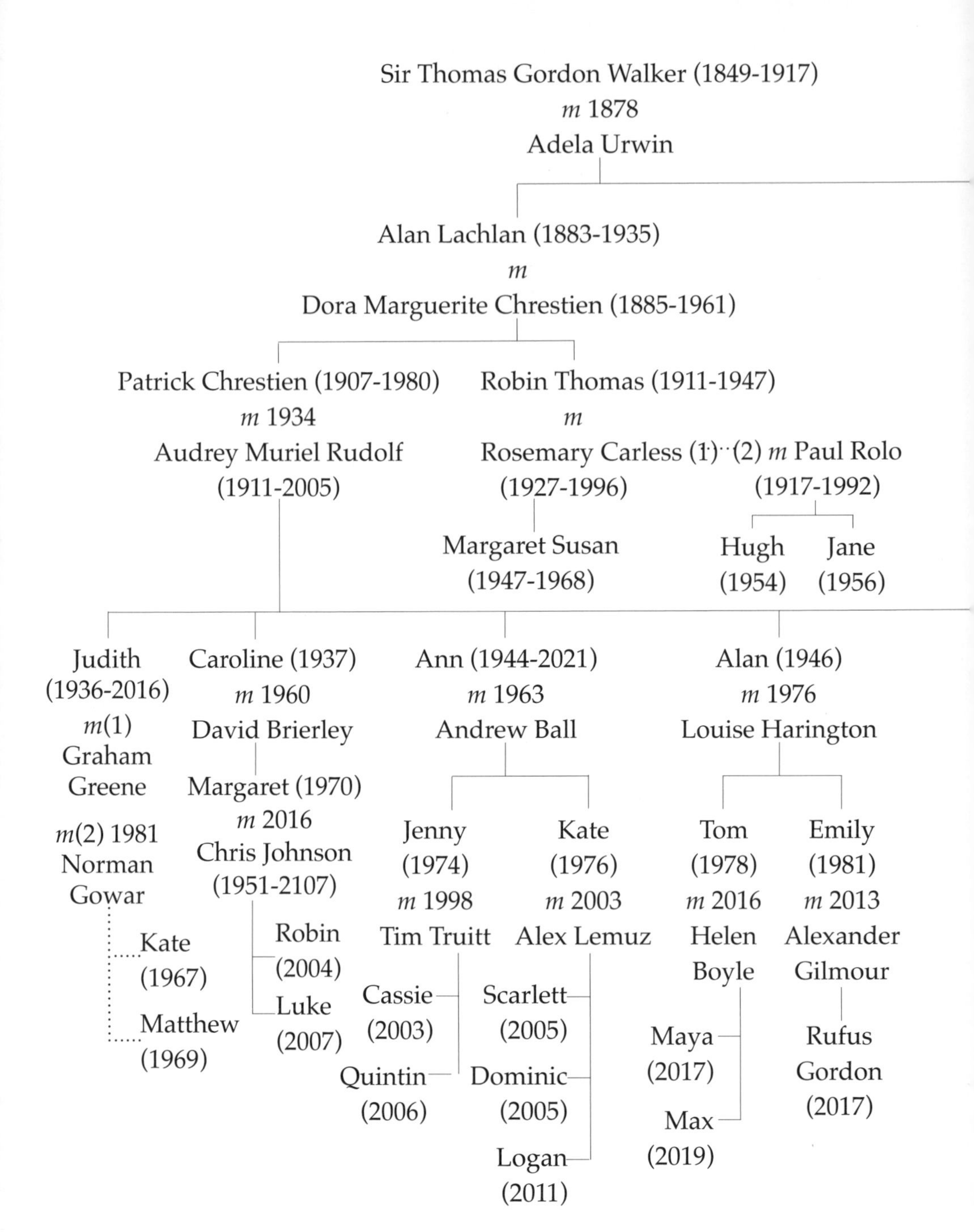

Sir Thomas Gordon Walker (1849-1917)
m 1878
Adela Urwin
Alan Lachlan (1883-1935)
m
Dora Marguerite Chrestien (1885-1961)
Patrick Chrestien (1907-1980)
m 1934
Audrey Muriel Rudolf
(1911-2005)
Robin Thomas (1911-1947)
m
Rosemary Carless (1) (2) m Paul Rolo
(1927-1996)
(1917-1992)
Margaret Susan
(1947-1968)
Hugh
(1954)
Jane
(1956)
Judith
(1936-2016)
m(1)
Graham
Greene
m(2) 1981
Norman
Gowar
Kate
(1967)
Matthew
(1969)
Caroline (1937)
m 1960
David Brierley
Margaret (1970)
m 2016
Chris Johnson
(1951-2107)
Robin
(2004)
Luke
(2007)
Ann (1944-2021)
m 1963
Andrew Ball
Jenny
(1974)
m 1998
Tim Truitt
Cassie
(2003)
Quintin
(2006)
Kate
(1976)
m 2003
Alex Lemuz
Scarlett
(2005)
Dominic
(2005)
Logan
(2011)
Alan (1946)
m 1976
Louise Harington
Tom
(1978)
m 2016
Helen
Boyle
Maya
(2017)
Max
(2019)
Emily
(1981)
m 2013
Alexander
Gilmour
Rufus
Gordon
(2017)

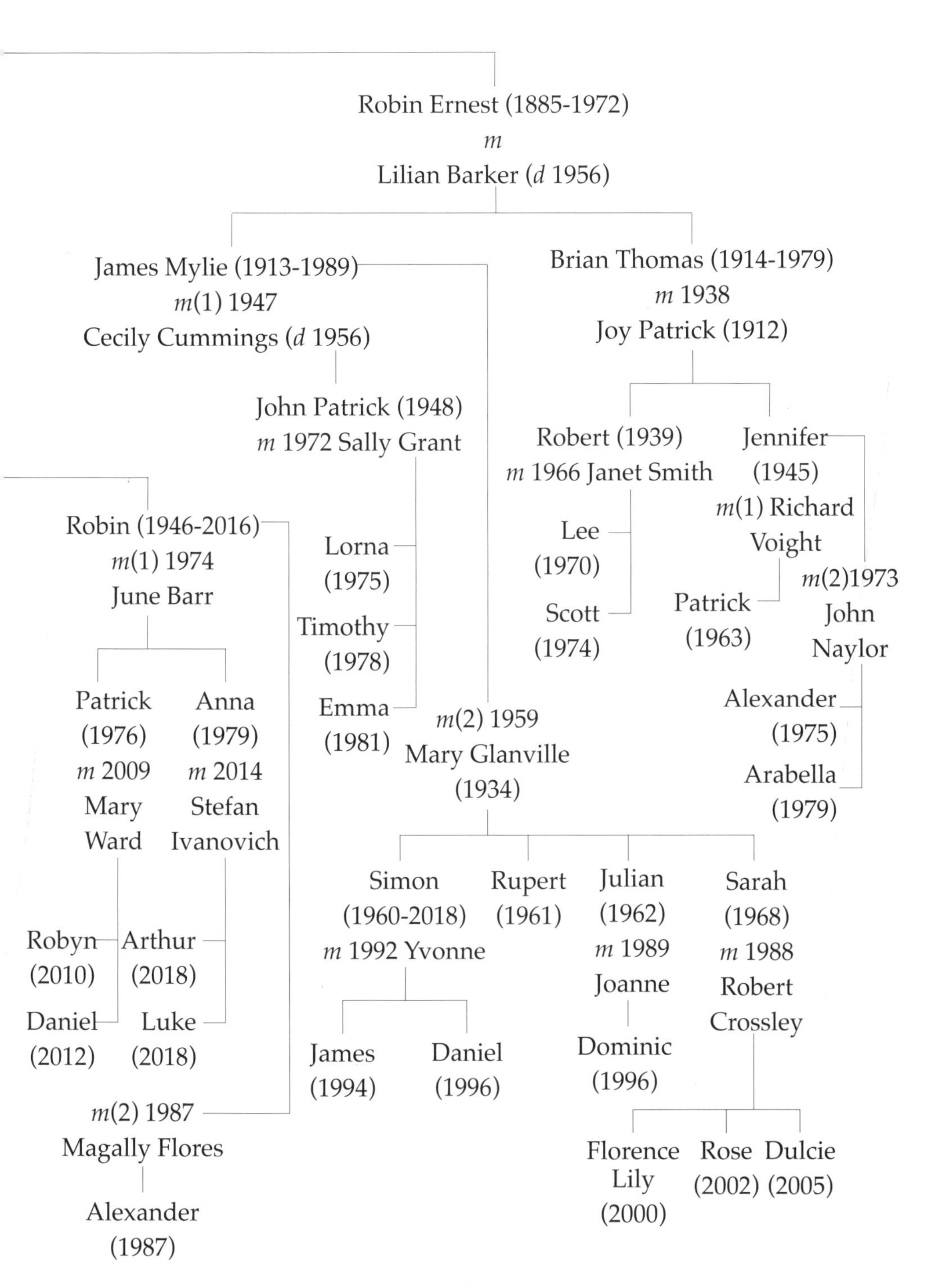
Robin Ernest (1885-1972)
m
Lilian Barker (*d* 1956)
James Mylie (1913-1989)
m(1) 1947
Cecily Cummings (*d* 1956)
Brian Thomas (1914-1979)
m 1938
Joy Patrick (1912)
John Patrick (1948)
m 1972 Sally Grant
Robert (1939)
m 1966 Janet Smith
Jennifer (1945)
m(1) Richard Voight
m(2)1973 John Naylor
Robin (1946-2016)
m(1) 1974
June Barr
Lorna (1975)
Timothy (1978)
Emma (1981)
Lee (1970)
Scott (1974)
Patrick (1963)
Alexander (1975)
Arabella (1979)
m(2) 1959
Mary Glanville (1934)
Patrick (1976) *m* 2009 Mary Ward
Anna (1979) *m* 2014 Stefan Ivanovich
Simon (1960-2018) *m* 1992 Yvonne
Rupert (1961)
Julian (1962) *m* 1989 Joanne
Sarah (1968) *m* 1988 Robert Crossley
Robyn (2010)
Daniel (2012)
Arthur (2018)
Luke (2018)
James (1994)
Daniel (1996)
Dominic (1996)
m(2) 1987
Magally Flores
Alexander (1987)
Florence Lily (2000)
Rose (2002)
Dulcie (2005)

Portrait by Feliks Topolski of Patrick Gordon Walker
as Shadow Foreign Secretary

Introduction

My father never wrote an autobiography, and we were never quite sure why this was. It may have been false modesty, a wish not to live in the past, or that the trauma of his political career made it painful to commit it all to paper. In his book *The Cabinet*, published in 1970, he included anecdotes and personal glimpses of the inner workings of power and described the cabinet in action – he served in three administrations, from 1950 to 1968. The thirty-year rule restricting the release of sensitive information applied to the first edition, limiting some parts that my father would have wished to include – now the thirty years are well past.

It seems right that his life should be recorded in a political and family biography, by one of his children, and the task has fallen to me. The book traces my father's life story, his political career and his role as a family man, devoted to his wife Audrey and to his five children. It has family photographs and is hopefully a fitting tribute to him.

My father's life (1907–1980) can be divided into four main parts, not all of the same length: India and schooldays; Christ Church, Oxford, as undergraduate and then student/don, and early politics; the war years at the BBC German Service; and member of Parliament in the Commons and then the Lords and Europe. His upbringing was conventional: his father was a judge in India, his mother's family, with French origins, was also conservative, and he went to an English prep school and to public school and then to one of the grandest Oxford colleges, Christ Church. It would perhaps have been more normal if he had been a Conservative, but fortunately he was not one. There must, however, have been contradictions in his life and maybe many did not understand the course he took: his mother certainly didn't, though she supported him financially all her life. Of course, in Oxford politics in the 1930s, the alternative to communism was fascism and this is the period when his views were formed. He was very far from being a communist, but this was an important reason that he and many intellectuals veered to the left, whatever their upbringing. The 1945 Labour government, it was said, contained more highly educated ministers than did Conservative administrations of the time, many of whom had gone straight into the services in the Second World War.

I know that I found, too, a confusion in my own life, with a similar conventional upbringing, but with a father in the Labour Party, and I was not surprised when I was gently approached at Oxford to see if I would like to 'serve my country', which I did not follow up, although I would have been a good spy. I remember that when Louise and I were going out together, we spent one day at a grand party through her family and the next week she was helping to call out the bingo numbers and, worse still, she had to sing the Red Flag in my father's constituency – hard for her parents, and probably her, to understand.

Certain family first names for male GWs occur time and again. Perhaps Robin is the most popular. There was Robin Ernest, my father's paternal uncle, Robin his brother and Robin his son. (My father was so keen on the name that when he registered the birth of me and my twin brother, he put us both down as Robin. I have an amendment from the registrar on my birth certificate to make me Alan!) Thomas is another name that occurs often: Sir Thomas, my father's grandfather; Robin Thomas, his brother; Brian Thomas Gordon Walker, my father's cousin, and his grandson Lee Thomas; and our son is Thomas too. My nephew, my brother's son, is Patrick like my father and his daughter is Robyn. One of the sons of my father's cousin Jim is John Patrick, and another cousin's son is Patrick Gordon. My grandfather was Alan Lachlan and I am Alan too. There are also a couple of Jameses.

The family is split between those who hyphenate our surname and those who do not. When my father went to the House of Lords, he had to hyphenate his name for the first time to become Lord Gordon-Walker. My family are Gordon Walker and our daughter Emily works as Emily Gordon Walker. My brother Robin's family are Gordon-Walker and his daughter Anna works as Anna Gordon-Walker. When my sisters Caroline and Ann, on divorce, reverted to their maiden name, they took Gordon-Walker, and Caroline's daughter Margaret is Margaret Gordon-Walker in her profession. My uncle Robin Thomas, like my father, had no hyphen. Jim Gordon Walker and his family do not hyphenate, whereas Brian Gordon-Walker and his family do. It seems to depend on if you want to be double-barrelled or have the option to be Walker, which is much more useful for booking tickets, airlines, restaurants and so on. There seem to be other Gordon Walkers who have been mentioned to us, particularly on the Isle of Wight, but the 'true' Gordon Walkers and Gordon-Walkers are known to us.

There is a streak of melancholia and sometimes of depression that runs through the Gordon Walkers and the Rudolfs, particularly in the male line. Almost everyone has times when they feel down – my wife Louise's father, in contrast, always saw each day as being better than the one before. My father had times when he was depressed but he belonged to a generation that did not talk openly about such things. My brother Robin certainly had his periods of black dog, sometimes quite severe: his sons perhaps have some of his symptoms in a mild way. My grandfather Norman Rudolf suffered from depression, as did his brother Vernon, Andrew Rudolf's father. My mother must have been affected by her family health afflictions. I am sure that such feelings must exist in most families.

For many people of my father's generation, the war years often meant a change of career. He was content in Oxford as a don and began his family there. He had already become involved in politics at Oxford, living and studying in Germany for a time during the first signs of the Nazi takeover, and without the war, his politics might have been less important than academia – but we will never know. My hunch is that he would have found his way more fully into politics than just in Oxford, but the war was the catalyst for change. In some ways, he was perhaps too academic for the cut and thrust of politics and some of his experiences in elections while at Oxford foreshadowed what was to come later. He was certainly extremely clever: he won a scholarship and gained a PhD, and was the author of five serious books. He read widely and he was fluent in German, which determined his wartime occupation and later produced much-needed income through German TV and radio, when he was trying to provide for five children on an MP's salary.

To his family and his wife, Audrey, he was always approachable, witty with a great sense of humour, a loving and supportive father to Judith, known to the family as Judy, Caroline, known as Carol, Ann, Robin and me. He read P.G. Wodehouse, *Three Men in a Boat* and *The Diary of a Nobody* to us and I only have the happiest memories of my father. He was Poppa to us all and to the grandchildren, only some of whom he knew. I am Poppa to my grandchildren, in tribute to him and because it is an easy word for children to say and remember. Sadly, there are only two of his children alive in 2022, Carol, who is in a nursing home, and me.

ONE

My Father's Family

My father's father, my grandfather Alan Lachlan (after whom I am named), was born in India in 1883. His parents were Thomas Walker, as he then was (later Sir Thomas), born in 1849, and Adela Irwin, daughter of the Rev. Alexander Irwin and Augusta Isabel Irwin, both of Scottish descent. They married in 1879. Adela was to play a part in my father's life. Thomas, whose middle name was Gordon, served in the Bengal Civil Service in Derba and Delhi and was awarded the Star of India. It appears that there were two Walkers in the civil service, so Thomas became Gordon Walker to distinguish them from each other. (This is more prosaic than the other suggestion that an earlier Alexander Walker married a Miss Gordon and they joined their names together to keep an inheritance.) Thomas Gordon Walker retired to Weybridge and died in 1917.

My father's grandmother, Adela, wife of Sir Thomas and taken in India.

Alan Lachlan fought in the First World War in Mesopotamia (later Iraq)

Alan Lachlan as a judge when he served in India. It is not clear whether this photograph encouraged or discouraged our daughter Emily from becoming the barrister and now judge which she is

After school and Balliol College, Oxford, his son Alan Lachlan returned to India in the Indian Civil Service – the premier civil service then – and spent most of his working life in India as a land settlement officer in the Punjab. During the First World War he served in Mesopotamia, now Iraq, reaching the rank of lieutenant-colonel. After the war, he worked in the hill station of Shimla and his last posting was as a judge in the supreme court of Lahore. This did not necessarily mean he was trained in law, because civil servants took on large areas of land and were responsible at a young age for justice and the well-being of the local population.

The Gordon Walkers' origins included the Gordons, the Lachlans, the Walkers and the Irwins, all prosperous Scottish families. These links were helpful to my Uncle Robin, my father's brother, when he was due to go to Balliol. There was a provision that, if you could trace your family back to John Balliol of Scotland, you could claim 'founder's kin' and get a free place. Uncle Robin managed to trace the family back to John Balliol's sister, so it was settled that he would get a fifty per cent deduction in fees – or so we were always told.

Alan Lachlan had a brother, Robin Ernest, born three years after him in 1886. Robin was in the Malay civil service and married Lillian Barker, who was born in 1884 and died in 1956. Their son, James, known as Jim, my father's cousin, was born in 1913, six years after my father. He married Cecily Cummings in 1946 and their eldest son, John Patrick, was born in 1947, a year after me and my twin Robin. Robin Ernest died in 1972, aged eighty-six, and Jim died in 1989, aged seventy-six. Cecily died in 1956, when they had only been married for ten years.

Alan Lachlan, my father's father, and my father's Uncle Robin, in sailor suits

Alan Lachlan with his wife Dora and carrying my father on his shoulder, circa 1909

Alan Lachlan married Dora Chrestien (1885–1961), whose family originally went to the subcontinent with the French East India Company, leaving from La Rochelle. La Rochelle was at that time a Huguenot redoubt, and Dora's family fluctuated between Calvin and Rome depending on the direction of the wind. Her brother Fernand Edward (F.E.) was a friend of Alan Lachlan and through him my grandfather met Dora, who looked very French – she was born in Marseilles – and several members of the family take after her in looks, with curly hair and a sallow complexion. F.E. (1882–1942) was a lawyer but he was only able to practise briefly as he became profoundly deaf in his mid- to late twenties, making him both diffident and difficult, and thereby forcing him to go and manage the family estates in Bihar in eastern India. He married Violet Howard, Aunt Violet, with whom we sometimes used to stay. Like Dora, she was born in 1885 and died in 1961. Dora's sister Marie Kate (1880–1957) married a Mr Dudley, whom we occasionally met. F.E. and Aunt Violet had three children; their son John (1902–1991) became a skilled painter, and we have a couple of his paintings. He came to stay with my parents along with his wife Charlotte, an American. John Chrestien, Jack Dudley and my father were all at St Ronan's prep school together.

John Chrestien's youngest sister, Diana de Beaufort, never married or had children. She worked for the Free French during the war and was based at the Lycée in South Kensington. After

Dora, my father's mother, carrying my father as a baby

the war she worked for my father as his private secretary, when he became an MP. She was godmother to my brother Robin and he kept up with that side of the family. She had a lengthy relationship with a Pole called Tadeusz Lisicki, who was involved with Bletchley Park and the breaking of the German codes. John Chrestien's second sister was Faye, who was born in 1910. She married Dick Partridge, a charming marine army officer who became a distinguished pilot, and they had two children, Simon and Penny. Simon, whose wife sadly died, was a good friend and kept in touch with Robin; we saw him at one stage regularly. We used to see Penny at family gatherings before she married and went to live in Greece.

Dora's family, the Chrestiens, lived in a grand house in Worthing, Tissre (named after one of the main bungalows on their Bihar estate, some of which are still there). The house was built in the 1870s or 1880s by Dora's father, Fernand François Chrestien (F.F.), born in 1838. It is still in existence and seems now to be owned by Worthing Council, but has alas, been turned into flats. It was very handsome and very large, and in

My father's maternal grandmother, Eliza Chrestien (neé Day), and the mother of Alan Lachlan's wife Dora

its pomp probably had grounds of some five to ten acres, with kitchen gardens, tennis courts and so on, all of which seem now to have been built upon. (I remember occasionally visiting my grandmother there with my parents.) F.F. was ensnared by a member of the 'Fishing Fleet', the ladies who went abroad to catch a suitable husband. He had wealth from the estates in Bihar, and he married Eliza Day, who was born in 1853. On his death in 1923, F.F.'s estate passed to F.E. As we have seen, F.F. had two daughters, Marie Kate and Dora, my father's mother, and there was also another son, Paul, who died in infancy. Eliza Day lived mainly at Tisree, at 14 Shakespeare Road, Worthing, while F.F. principally lived in India. Eliza died in 1933 and Dora then took on Tisree and it became the family home for my father, his brother Robin and his father, Alan Lachlan.

Dora returned to England for the birth of both of her sons, my father Patrick Chrestien on 7 April 1907 and his brother Robin

My father with his brother, taken in Worthing, where the family lived when not in India

My father aged 8, in school clothes with his brother Robin

My father around 10 years old

My father and Robin, aged around 11 and 5

Thomas in 1910, rather than having them locally in India. (This was fortunate, as my mother was born in Jamaica; if my father had died first, as he did, my mother would have had difficulty in proving her right to keep living in England. As it was, there was still pressure after my father died to send her back to Jamaica, which was overcome by family influence from her children.) My father and his brother spent their early years in India with their parents, but they were sent back to England to school, firstly at a conventional preparatory school, St Ronan's, and then at Wellington College in the 1920s, my father from 1921 to 1925. Both my father and Uncle Robin were clever and also excelled at sport – rugby, hockey, cricket and tennis – as well as academically. Schools were tougher in those days, but both seemed to accept the routine at prep school and then at Wellington and seemed to flourish there, playing in the top teams and being house and college prefects.

My father was subeditor of the Wellington College magazine, his first foray into writing that was to continue all his life. He was a company sergeant-major in the Officers' Training Corps, head of his house, the Hardinge, and one of the half-dozen who won a scholarship to Oxbridge. In 1925 he was awarded an open scholarship to Christ Church, Oxford. Robin went to Balliol and subsequently taught at Wellington in the 1930s and became tutor of the Hardinge: the two brothers' paths were to cross in the war. When my twin brother and I were in our turn suddenly sent to Wellington from a day prep school, we were less successful, looking up to every board listing the sporting or academic achievements of P.C. Gordon Walker and R.T. Gordon Walker. On the surface they appeared happy, but the treatment of children in those days, and the need for them to stand on their own feet, meant that children did not complain – and certainly not to their parents.

My Uncle Robin around the time of leaving Wellington en route to Balliol. Both he and my father lost their hair in their twenties

My father was nineteen and just going up to Oxford when the General Strike of 1926 broke out. It was a momentous time when university students took sides as to whether to support the workers or to keep the country going. My father had yet to become involved in politics and he told me that he remained neutral, but his instincts were to have supported the striking workers.

My grandmother Dora (Dodo) was not maternal and had coolish relations when they were growing up with my father and Uncle Robin – in those days children tended to be looked after by nurses and to be seen and not heard. The relations of my father and uncle with their parents were especially distant as they were in India. The boys were sent back early to prep school, as was the custom, and in the holidays they were farmed out to grandparents and other relatives. My father would recount stories of his eccentric paternal grandmother Adela, of throwing a cake over the roof and reciting to the brothers that she would

Adela at a more mature age. My father and his brother Robin often stayed with their grandparents while their own parents were in India

rather keep them for a week than a fortnight. Every four years or so, either the boys would sail out to India to see their parents – a journey of several months – or their mother would return to England. It seems a strange life now, but was quite normal at that time, before quick means of transport allowed regular visits home, and continued with annual visits for many schoolchildren until the 1970s. The last time my father went to India, he found that his parents' marriage had deteriorated. They were leading separate lives, as was often the case in India then, but appeared to be together for form's sake.

No-one talked about it, but there seems to have been infidelity on both sides. In the stifling summer, the wives and children went up to the hills in Shimla and there was temptation for the men left behind working. Divorce was out of the question for it would ruin careers, even if relations were strained. I remember my father telling me that when he returned to India for his last visit, his mother sent him away, as she did not want to admit to being old enough to have such a grown-up son, harming her chances with her gentlemen callers – maybe an apocryphal story.

At various stages, there was unrest in India, and it was discovered that there was a plot on the life of my grandfather Alan Lachlan: maybe he was too tough on the local population. The Indian civil service feared that any disturbance would be a distraction and a threat to their authority. My grandfather reluctantly resigned as a judge at the early age of forty-eight – 'I see', he wrote, 'that the shooting of a judge would not ease the political situation and I do not wish to embarrass the Government in any way.' He stayed on for a while to take his leave and then took a leisurely journey 'home' to England, by boat and overland to Paris. It is not clear if Dora was with him, or whether she had returned earlier. My parents went to Paris to meet him and while there, his appendix burst, and he died of peritonitis on 16 September 1932. In those days there was little that could be done. He was just over fifty years old.

Dora would later remarry a Colonel Leslie Kent, who had served in India, so I guess they knew each other before, but how well history does not recount. My father would recite how, at her second marriage, he walked his mother down the aisle. Colonel Kent had torn the baize of the only billiard table in the mess in India and was thereafter known as 'Cutter' Kent, though not to his face. We were told to call him Step, but this was later changed to Poppa Leslie, which did not catch on. When we occasionally went to Tisree with our parents, I recall Dora and 'Cutter' Kent as being severe and not used to children, as they had always had servants to look after them, or they were away at school. Visiting them in their house at 14 Shakespeare Road, Worthing, where my

Uncle Robin escorting his mother, Dora, to a wedding

Dora and her second husband, Colonel Leslie Kent, on the way to a wedding

father had been born and they now lived, was always an ordeal and a journey not often undertaken. Dora was certainly well off and often came financially to the rescue of her son's increasing family, until she died in June 1961. (When my sister Carol moved a few years ago into a nursing home in Worthing, it was one street away from Shakespeare Road and, when we visited her, we identified where the family home had been.)

TWO

My Mother's Family

Whereas my father's family was sedate and conservative, my mother, Audrey Rudolf, came from a Jamaican family that was perhaps more unconventional than the Gordon Walkers. Both her parents' families had lived in Jamaica for generations, her father's having originally come from Scotland. My grandfather Norman Andrew Rudolf (known as Grampie when my grandparents came to live with us after the war) was the eldest of eight, born in 1883, and my grandmother Frederica Ann Solomon (Didi to us) was the youngest of eight, born in 1888. Grampie's siblings were Edna, Alzie, Oscar, Oswald, Harry (whom we used to see with his family in London and whose daughter Kiki, with whom we are still in touch, often came to stay), Vernon and Elsie, married to Clemy. Many of the Rudolfs did not marry and some lost potential husbands in the First World War, where Uncle Oscar was killed in 1918, fighting with the Canadian army – there were close ties between the two countries.

My great-grandfather on the Rudolf side was Henry James, who married a Helen Mossman. When we went to live in Sydney in the 1980s, we lived in Mosman, reputedly named after the Jamaican ancestors, who had been whalers – spelling was not a fixed art in those days.

My cousin Andrew Rudolf, the son of my grandfather Norman's youngest brother, Vernon, produced an extensive family tree of the Rudolfs, to which my grandfather strenuously objected. 'Don't meddle where you should not go,' he admonished Andrew. One can see why, as there were some eccentric forebears and several children born on the wrong side of the blanket, including, I was told, a liaison with the Queen of St Kitts. Andrew has been a long-standing friend and valued member of the extended family.

My grandmother's side of the family was descended from Solomon Solomons (1784–1866). There were eight siblings: my grandmother Frederica, George, Eve, Rachel, Con, Marie, David and Fred. Rachel married a Mr MacFarlane, whose daughter Doreen came into our life later. Con married a Mr Bower and had a daughter, Sheila, whom we saw at various occasions and who left money to three of Didi's grandchildren, me, Ann and Robin.

Didi's brother George Solomon Solomons was mayor of Kingston. He was an important figure and was knighted and subsequently changed his name to become Sir George Seymour Solomon and then Sir George Seymour Seymour, to sound less Jewish, which in those days was a hindrance to progress. The irony is that Seymour also has Jewish undertones, as I knew

My grandfather's family, the Rudolfs in Jamaica, around 1902-3.
Back row, left to right. *Oscar (killed in the First World War fighting with the Canadian armies), Norman, my mother's father, Edna, Oswald and Harry.*
Second row, left to right. *Vernon (Andrew Rudolf's father) Helen Rudolf nee Mossman and Henry James Rudolf. Alzie is sitting at the front.*
When Judy, Carol and cousin Andrew were evacuated in the Second World War, they spent time with the Rudolf and Solomon families

My mother's Uncle George in Jamaica. He was an important figure, being mayor, gaining a knighthood and running racehorses. He changed his name from George Solomon Solomon to Sir George Seymour Seymour

when I was at school in London, and we went swimming in St John's Wood at the Seymour Baths. He was a keen racehorse owner and there was a Seymour racing cup. I have a gold miniature of one of the racing cups that he won.

The love of Uncle George's life was Evelyn Burke, but he could only marry her when her husband died. She had two daughters, Madge and Olive, who lived with her and Uncle George. Madge married a Mr Salter, known as 'Tarzan' – nobody remembers why – and they had two children, William, who died at twelve, and Penny. Penny later came to London and met and married an English soldier, Vic Higgs. He was sent off to serve abroad and his mother made it clear that she was reluctant to have someone from Jamaica to stay. Penny therefore lodged with us and helped my father with secretarial work when he was an MP. She has remained a life-long friend.

My grandfather Norman was a not very successful plantation owner. There were estates which were later to increase greatly in value through tourism, in areas of the island including Montego Bay, though sadly after the family had lost possession of them. He went to the Ontario Agricultural College at Guelph in Canada, gaining a BSc: the college specialised in agriculture and land management. He wrote articles on agriculture and growing crops, which appeared in the *Jamaican*. Much later they were collected together in a short book he published called *The Fruitful Earth: Tropical Agriculture without Tears*. He was not always as successful as his writings indicated and there were often moves to new plantations. Agriculture was difficult in Jamaica with hurricanes hitting the banana trees, and in the Second World War, Britain switched from sugar cane to sugar beet grown at home. The trouble was that there was never enough capital to invest properly in the land.

Norman and Frederica had a stillborn child, Norma, and then my mother, Audrey Muriel, born on Christmas Eve 1911, and her brother Neville, born in 1913. I know little of their upbringing in Jamaica, but they were both clever and academic. The relationship between my mother's parents was not good, not helped by my grandfather's deafness – communications often seemed to be conducted through their children. My grandfather's first course on moving to a new plantation, we were told – perhaps as a joke – was to clear land for a tennis court, rather than for planting crops. He was fanatical about tennis and played as often as he could. History relates that he played mixed doubles with a woman twice in succession, which was deemed to be akin to adultery, and his wife is rumoured to have never spoken to him again while they lived in Jamaica. When later they lived with our family in Hampstead after the war, he still played tennis and never missed watching Wimbledon in black and white on our small TV set. (Being deaf, he had a choice of putting his ear-trumpet to the sound, but missing the picture, or sitting further away and seeing but not hearing – how he would have loved today's televisions.)

My mother, Audrey, aged about 2

My grandmother was a strong and determined woman, minute in stature but ruling the roost. She had a favourite child, and it was not my mother, but Neville, who could do no wrong. (When my mother was in her dotage in a nursing home, and living mostly in the past, she asked me which of my two children was my favourite. She did not believe me when I said I had no favourite, but being the second choice for her own mother, Didi, was deeply embedded in her psyche.) Neville went to London University and was to live in South Africa with his wife Joan. Neville was against apartheid, but they still lived well with servants. He was high up in Gypsum Industries. We saw them from time to time on visits and they were an entertaining couple. They sadly could not have children but adopted two girls, Nicola and Penny – Penny died a few years ago. The only way they could get money out of South Africa, where there were stringent currency controls, was to buy a boat. Neville was a keen sailor and they reached Portugal, where they sold the boat to pay for their retirement, in a country which had a similar warm climate to the one that they were used to.

Though she had little education, Didi knew what she wanted and was determined to give her children the very best. My mother went to Hampton Girls' School, which was always to play an important part in her life. There she did well and made friends. She was excellently taught by teachers often from Britain and flourished, especially under the Scottish headmistress, Miss Agnes Campbell, who took her under her wing and became a life-long friend when she retired to England. My brother and I once took her boating on the Thames near Reading, where she was at a senior age living in a convent at Caversham. She ended up with one foot in the boat and one on the land, with fateful results; she was very wet and we did not know what to do, as we tried not to laugh out loud. We got her home, but it took a long time for our mother to forgive us.

My mother won the annual Jamaica scholarship awarded by Oxford University, like a Rhodes scholarship; there was one for men and one for women. This was a great achievement, and she set off in 1929, aged just under eighteen, to a new life thousands of miles away from home and her favoured brother Neville. It was a frightening move and quite a wrench coming to Oxford, where there were few women at the university. She was found digs at the hostel for home students in what later became St Anne's. Life there was chaperoned and controlled as she studied at the university; she read English, one of the few degrees open to women then. She had been top of her class in Jamaica, but Oxford was a different matter, and she found it all a pressure. Although she had been well taught, she had not read all the books for her course and was behind many of the British undergraduates academically. She had been brought up to be on her best behaviour and to be of good stature. My mother worked very hard but meeting my father cannot have helped her studies and she only got a low degree, which knocked her confidence further and perhaps give her a feeling of inferiority thereafter, which affected her all her life. She had a clever husband and was part of a family that was mainly to excel academically.

THREE

Oxford Together

My father had a successful time at Christ Church. He continued to play rugby, narrowly missing a blue, and studied hard. He did not quite attain the expected First in history in 1928, but this was mitigated by being awarded the Gladstone Memorial Exhibition in the following year and a degree of BLitt in 1931 for a thesis on the National Debt. He then became a student (that is a don) teaching European history. He was quite a swell and went around in either a purple velvet corduroy suit and a yellow shirt – or the other way round.

Patrick aged around 23, at Christ Church

My father with friends skiing in Austria. There were no lifts in those days

With this position as a don in Oxford came some status and importance. Christ Church, the 'House', was a major college and among his fellow dons were Sir Keith Filing, Gilbert Murray, Gilbert Ryle, Roy Harrod and the 'Prof' himself, Frederick Lindemann, later Lord Cherwell. There seemed no reason why he should not continue to live the civilised life of an Oxford academic and to produce elegant and erudite works of high scholarship.

My father spent much of 1930 in Germany, becoming fluent in the language, reading for a doctorate. On one visit in 1932, he was in Berlin when Chancellor von Papen dismissed the Prussian government and proclaimed martial law. He saw Goebbels speaking at Nuremberg, warming up the crowd for Adolf Hitler. Familiarity with Germany brought him into close contact with the British Labour Party, who used him to make contact with oppressed German social democrats and trade unionists, who were among groups which were already deemed a threat to a proposed totalitarian government.

My parents had both been in Oxford and we always believed that they first met at the Air Squadron Ball, of which my father was a member. There is a photograph of him as the book's frontispiece, resplendent in sheepskin flying jacket, with the inevitable pipe and already thinning on top, though he was only thirty-seven (my twin brother, Robin, lost his hair at the same age). My mother had been soberly brought up, already religious, so history does not recount how well they knew each other before their marriage. My father was quite a catch – a handsome don, clever and well connected and making a name for himself. They were married on 21 December 1934, at a ceremony at Caxton Hall, London, my father in a suit and my mother in a polka dot dress. (There is a photo of this on the opposite page.) We were told that because my mother was planning to return to Jamaica to be a teacher – always the intention – my father realised that he had better rouse himself and propose, so there was no time to arrange conventional wedding clothes, a church wedding or a large ceremony. Perhaps few people attended, as most of my mother's family were in Jamaica. My father's best man was an Oxford friend, Dunstan Skilbeck; he would become principal of Wye Agricultural College, later a part of London University. My father was not religious, but my mother certainly was and continued to be so all her life. They returned to their new Oxford home in Museum Road, a small road by the Parks, still there now. It was close enough to Christ Church, where my father kept his rooms for teaching in Canterbury Quad, just off Peckwater, where I would have rooms thirty years later. He said he was pleased not to be living permanently in college, though he still dined at High Table, with the likes of W. H. Auden and other famous students.

During this period, when they were just married, sometime in 1935, my mother went on a visit to Germany with my father, to meet an underground socialist movement. Trade unionists were already coming to the attention of the German police and civil authorities, a foretaste of what was to come. This was a journey fraught with danger and my mother provided some

My parents' wedding in London, 21 December 1934. The story was that my mother was set to return to Jamaica as a teacher, having given up on my father. Realising the urgency, he proposed and my mother did not have time to find a wedding dress. They look a fine couple and my mother very beautiful

A stylised photo of my mother, in Oxford soon after her marriage

cover of a seemingly innocent married couple on holiday. They were nearly arrested at a flat which had been taken over by the Gestapo. My mother in later life, when her short-term memory was going, told me that they wanted to get some threatened trade unionists out of a house guarded by the police. My mother, who was very pretty, went to the front of the house and adjusted her garter to distract the guards, while my father and those they were aiding escaped out of the back door. They all got to a train and made their escape, nervous of capture the whole way home. My mother was pregnant with her first child, Judith, and this provided some cover – she also hid some documents under her clothes by her bump.

My father's upbringing could not have been more conservative and conventional, with the family links to India and attending a major public school. He explained that there were two reasons for his life-long commitment to the Labour Party. One was that, before the welfare state, there was real poverty, with little unemployment dole and no universal NHS. One in principle only saw a doctor if one could pay for it, though it was believed that many doctors soaked the rich to treat the poor. The second was that the alternative to communism and the left was fascism and the right. He was never a communist, but he sided with the left, though later, after the war, he was to track to the right of the party.

In the 1930s my father was now embedded in the Labour Party, writing and attending meetings. German trade unionists, escaping from the authorities, were always found a welcome with my parents in Museum Road. In 1935, he published his first book, *The Sixteenth and Seventeenth Centuries*, which came from the subjects he taught and studied; he was still a full-time don and his research and teaching was as important as politics. In June 1936, Oswald Mosley came to speak in Oxford and the Labour Party organised opposition. My father gave his reason for joining the party thus: 'The Conservatives have degraded the country and I wanted to be proud of it.' The year of his marriage he was secretary of the Oxford University Labour Party, while another old Wellingtonian, F.B.D. Fitzgerald-Moore, was president of the Oxford University Fascist Association – my father had travelled a long way from Crowthorne, Berkshire, the home of Wellington College.

In 1935, my father became Labour's official candidate for the city of Oxford in the general election. There was only a slim chance of winning and this was 'more of a flag-waving exercise against hopeless odds'. Stalwarts like Harold Laski, Douglas Cole, Dick Crossman and Elizabeth Pakenham (married to Frank, also a don at Christ Church) supported him. His policies railed against the Means Test and the fact that sixty per cent of Britain's earned less than £122 a year and half of the nation's income went to only ten per cent of the population (little seems to have changed in my father's analysis of the distribution of wealth when inflation is taken into account). He polled 9,661 votes to the Conservatives' 16,306 – perhaps a foretaste of the elections he was to lose in the 1960s. At this stage his policies were radical, though he did not yet see the need for extensive rearmament – his views were to change after the Anschluss and the growing threat of the fascists. He had seen first-hand the threat from Germany and Hitler.

Political parties have always been broad coalitions of a wide spectrum of differing interests. The Labour Party was more to the left than it became and veered towards communism and trade unionism, from which the party was born. It was only later that some members moved to the right. The Conservative Party had elements that shared views with the fascists, though most members were more conventionally in the middle of the

The wedding of my mother's brother, Neville, to Joan Harcourt. My parents are accompanied by the bride's mother

political orbit. Having seen the evils of fascism with his own eyes, it was not surprising that my father veered leftwards, notwithstanding his background and family.

In January 1936, Judith, my eldest sister, was born and in December 1937, Caroline followed. The young family moved from Museum Road to a house rented in Boar's Hill at Garsington called Pettywell. My father loved family life and always adored young children, including grandchildren to come. It was a happy time in their life.

My father's political and academic life took much of his time. Captain Bourne, who had beaten my father in the election in 1935, died in August 1938 and my father was due to stand again. By now there was much debate and a clear difference of policy about appeasement to Hitler. The Conservatives attacked Labour's policy of support for standing up to fascism, which had spread to Spain from Italy and Germany, saying that it meant flirting with communism. Rearmament was now a major topic, supported by Labour, with which my father now agreed. In the build-up to the by-election, there were certainly pockets of communism in Oxford and Frank Pakenham supported a Popular Front man as candidate. My father fought hard to remain as the Labour candidate, but there were strong feelings among Oxford dons, some of them friends of my father. When the Liberal candidate was persuaded to stand down by Roy Harrod, a fellow don at Christ Church, to avoid splitting the vote, my father was similarly forced to stand aside, which he did with extreme reluctance: 'I am not standing down. The local Labour Party is withdrawing the Labour candidate.' It was another bitter blow for him, a foretaste perhaps of what was to come.

A. D. Lindsay, the master of Balliol, became the new candidate to replace my father and fight against the Conservative candidate, Quintin Hogg, later Lord Hailsham. Lindsay was not an experienced political figure, though backed by Crossman and Pakenham – showing again that there are no friends in politics, even though Frank and Elizabeth Pakenham, later Lord

My father in a posed portrait just before the Second World War

and Lady Longford, were personal friends of my parents, each couple being godparents to the other's children, and later the families lived a few doors from each other. (I had the misfortune to have to publish Lord Longford's pornography report in 1972.) The election was won by Hogg, who saw it as a victory for appeasement, as Hogg described it. He received 15,797 votes to Lindsay's 12,363, so not a convincing victory.

My father, despite being stood down, continued to support the Labour Party, canvassing in local elections and also working for the National Council for Labour Colleges, a rather unfashionable body which provided correspondence courses for rank-and-file trade unionists. In 1939 he published his second book, *An Outline of Man's History*, a thoughtful history of man from the emergence of *Homo sapiens* to the upheavals of the 1930s. It was dedicated to the workers: 'They', he wrote, 'are, more than any class, able to approach history with honesty, clarity and freedom from inhibitions.'

FOUR

The War Years: 1939–1945

Oxford at the beginning of the Second World War remained calm and serene. High Table continued, but with perhaps fewer courses at dinner. My father was still politically active. He and A. J. P. Taylor led a campaign to aid the thousands of refugees from the East End as Londoners were evacuated before a bomb had been dropped. They organised entertainments and some were put up in the family house in Garsington. He was involved with the Oxford University Labour Club, but in 1940 it was expelled by the National Executive Committee (NEC). Its members then formed the Oxford University Democratic Socialist Club. G. D. H. Cole was president, Anthony Crosland was chairman and Roy Jenkins was treasurer – perhaps a foretaste of the Social Democratic Party of the 1980s.

My father had fallen foul of the incipient Nazi government through his activity helping German social democrat trade unionists in the early 1930s, aiding them to come to England and putting some up in Oxford. For this reason, he was told that he was on the Nazi 'blacklist' if Germany invaded, which in 1940 seemed more than likely. My grandmother's Solomon family would also have been sufficient for my mother and her children to be deemed Jewish enough to be in danger of a concentration camp. There was also the expectation that London would be bombed. Many children had been evacuated and then returned but for Judy and Carol there was an alternative in Jamaica where my mother's parents and many relations still were. Pressure also came from Vola Rudolf, married to one of my grandfather's brothers, Uncle Vernon. They lived in central London with their son, Andrew, who was the same age as Judy and Carol, albeit of a different generation.

Vola was particularly keen on getting Andrew away, even though he was a Rudolf (and not a Solomon) and neither his parents nor he were on any blacklist. She wrote in her handwriting to my mother in mid-May 1940, just before Dunkirk (27 May–4 June) when the Allied forces were in full retreat:

> My dear Audrey,
>
> Just a note written to you in despair! Have you any plans at all? If only we could get the children out to Jamaica, but I suppose even that is too late.
>
> Mother [Vola's mother] has taken Andrew & my niece [her sister's daughter] to North Somerset, so they are safe for the moment. But for how long? I wonder how you feel about things & whether you have any plans. Do write a note if you have the heart & the time. We will win in the end, but at what a price or are we going to lose? I am quite despondent & heartsick for the young lives lost in France.
>
> With love to you all.
>
> Vola
>
> If there is anything I can do, or if you have any suggestions, do let me know.

Discussion continued and eventually the momentous decision was made for the three children to go together to Jamaica for a few months until the threat of invasion and bombing was over. Judy, Carol and Andrew left in late June 1940 on the Camito. Judy was four and a half years old, Andrew three and a half and little Carol only two and a half. They were accompanied by a nurse, Eileen Campling, specially chosen for the voyage, who returned back home as soon as she had delivered her charges. She subsequently married a fireman, John D'Almeida, who lived near us after the war, and he did odd jobs for my father when he was not on duty.

It was a catastrophic decision. The war that was of course to be over by Christmas – as are all wars – continued until 1945

My parents at Pettywell, Oxford, around 1939, with Judith and Caroline, about a year before they were evacuated to Jamaica.

and U-boat activity meant that no civilians could return for five years. Imagine how it must have felt to all involved: no-one ever contemplated such a long and disastrous separation. One can only surmise what my father and mother thought of what they had set in train. It seems to have been partly 'out of sight, out of mind'. Letters took months to arrive, and my father sent a mixture of his own stories and Kipling stories. My sisters and Andrew did not know which were which. Judy and Carol stayed with their grandparents Didi and Grampie at a home called Orchard, though they were also running a small hotel at Montego Bay called Ma Vista, then totally undeveloped. Orchard was on pretty rocky terrain and started as a sugar plantation, but as the weather got dryer, it was switched to coconuts and pimento. The lack of tourists and the switch in agriculture at Orchard meant there was little income coming in, but Judy and Carol were well looked after and cared for.

The original plan was for all three to stay at Ma Vista or Orchard, but Andrew, on his own and with the nurse returning home, was traumatised by the evacuation and was rather difficult. The decision was taken for Andrew to go to Hampstead, where his uncle Oswald (Ozzie) lived with the maiden aunts Alzie and Edna. As Andrew proved hard to handle – his own words – he was sent to Frontier, Port Maria, where his aunt Elsie lived with her husband Clemy. Elsie managed to find an English nanny for Andrew, Beryl King, who had been stranded in Jamaica. Andrew later had a spell at Montego Bay with Judy and Carol and went to Mrs Clegg's school at Appleton Hall. He was still based with his uncle and aunts, but spent some time with his cousins and their grandparents. Carol and Andrew also attended the junior department of the Montego High School for Girls. Andrew then boarded at Hill Crest in Brown Town for six months in 1944, to get him used to returning home, so the three of them were together for quite a part of the time.

Judy became a surrogate mother to her younger sister, a control and dependence which continued all their lives. The others were too young to take it all in, but Judy was the most affected and never really re-established a satisfactory relationship with our mother when they finally returned. It seems unbelievable now, but wartime meant decisions had to be made which would otherwise make no sense. How much easier it would have been if only our grandparents had lived in the West Country.

My parents were living in London and renting a flat in Vicarage Road in Kensington. My mother, free of childcare, could throw herself into the war effort. She was an intelligent, university-educated 29-year-old. She joined the censorship office, reading letters to and from soldiers fighting abroad or in the UK, to remove any sensitive information which could endanger the war effort. She was a supervisor in a factory which made parachutes, checking that they had been packed properly – literally a matter of life and death. She also took her turn helping in London Underground stations used as shelters in the Blitz, looking after

My father in military uniform around 1940, in the garden of Pettywell near Oxford

children and providing refreshment for what could be all-night sessions. She often said, even when her daughters had returned from exile, that the war had been the best part of her life – hardly tactful. What she meant was that with men fighting or being in the services, there was a unique role for women, as civilians or in the services themselves – one which was to disappear to a large extent when the boys came home.

My parents had moved to Northmoor Road in North Oxford, in March 1939. The children were staying with Chrestien relations before being evacuated, to keep them in the country, and my parents took in a family evacuated from the East End. My father's time in the war was to be more cerebral, and he was looking around for a role involved in the war effort. In 1940, he was thirty-three, but although he had been high up in the Combined Cadet Force (CCF) at Wellington, he was better suited for a non-combatant role. Quintin Hogg suggested a role

My father in 1940, still at Oxford before he joined the BBC German service

at the Ministry of Economic Welfare, but it was not to be. After some effort, he found a niche at the European Service of the BBC, where his fluent German was a boon. This necessitated my parents' move to London, notwithstanding the Blitz to come. Occasional broadcast talks by my father led to a permanent placement under Hugh Carleton Greene, later a progressive director general of the BBC, whose son was to marry my sister Judy seventeen years later. My father had already had a taste of German propaganda in a week's trip to Germany in 1938. He had seen the German propaganda machine in full action on the Czech crisis, so he knew first-hand how formidable the German broadcasts could be. He managed and wrote broadcasts to Germany, of course in German.

Seeing the outright propaganda used by Goebbels and Lord Haw-Haw, the decision was made to be more honest in broadcasts and season them with a leavening of truth about setbacks, in the expectation that, when things got better, they were more likely to be believed. German listeners tended to be impressed by the quiet tone of the BBC broadcasts given by my father and others and gave credence to accounts of bad days and good. The daily schedule began early morning, and they had a large audience, despite the dangers of listening abroad to the BBC. My father gave a topical talk on the Beveridge Report and this formed part of a broadcast. It was serious work and the teams felt that they had a real sense of responsibility. My father, perhaps to excite us, used later to say that sometimes they were asked to use certain phrases in their broadcasts aimed at the resistance in Europe about RAF drops of men and supplies. This may not have been the case – but we were impressed as children by it anyway.

My father's younger brother Robin had returned from Balliol to teach history at Wellington, becoming tutor of the Hardinge, the house that they had both been in at their time at school, as well as head of history. He was a charismatic and popular teacher and loved by those he taught or looked after in his house. Perhaps he was too popular and too loved. As many schoolmasters were away at the war, there was a divide between the old teachers who could not fight and those too young to do so. My Uncle Robin had a weak heart and could not join up. Of course, Wellington being an army school, the older boys were keen when they left to join up after basic training.

Some, particularly 'old guard' teachers, may have thought that my uncle was too close to students with whom he came into contact and certainly his methods were collegiate. He sided with the chaplain about giving succour to the boys who needed it. Wellington was quite tough then and was still so when my brother and I were there decades later. Great store was set on hearty games. Robin and the chaplain, Geofrey How, encouraged boys to have friends in other houses, something frowned on then, and still when we were there, because who knew where it would lead? The headmaster, Bobby Longdon, who would have helped to heal the divisions and splits in Common Room, was killed by a stray bomb and his replacement was too weak to stand up to the

Uncle Robin as a teacher at Wellington College with two members of his house towering over him. He recounted his time at Wellington in a roman à clef, Path of Duty

teachers. Seeking a quiet life, in 1943 he dismissed the chaplain, and to his surprise, and disappointment, Robin resigned too.

Robin later wrote a fictionalised version of what had happened, in 1944, a year after he had left, which lay in a drawer until my brother and I found it. I published this as *Path of Duty* in 2015, over seventy years after the events described. (The gates put up at Wellington in Robin's memory had the motto 'The Path of Duty is the Way to Glory'.) In 1943, Robin needed a job, and with help from his brother, he joined the BBC propaganda service, where my father was playing a key role.

This stage of the war demanded close Allied co-operation in the build up to D-Day and my father's work was to be increasingly alongside the Americans. Together they created a Psychological Warfare Division (PWD). When the American troops reached Luxembourg in late 1944, after the advance following D-Day, they acquired Radio Luxembourg, as the

Germans had failed to destroy it. My father with two others were sent out to Luxembourg to run the transmitter. Thereafter it became a base and there is a photograph with BBC colleagues there, including my father and brother Robin in army uniform. (After the war, Radio Luxembourg could reach the UK for broadcasts, circumventing the BBC monopoly, as the mast had been strengthened in its reach for the BBC wartime transmissions home, and was listened to on crystal sets under the bedclothes.)

My father kept diaries of this important time and he described life in war-riven Luxembourg, arriving on 21 October 1944 to a rapturous welcome from those who had regularly tuned into BBC programmes. His most celebrated broadcasts, however, were when he visited Germany twice with a recording van. He was given the rank of an honorary major, so that he could use the officers' mess on US bases. He described to his children that he had been going along a road and stopped to ask the way of the crew of a US jeep and whether it was safe to proceed. They laconically replied that it was probably unwise, as there was a German tank round the corner. The BBC recording van quickly changed tack. The first trip was from 24 February to 1 March 1945, crossing the river Roer a few days after the first Allied troops entered the area around Aachen. On 24 February at Bastogne, on the Belgium–Luxembourg border, there seemed to be hardly a house standing and the team went through ruined towns and desolation everywhere. He succeeded in getting civilians to make broadcasts suggesting that their relatives should desert from the Wehrmacht.

His second trip into Germany was from 16 to 23 April 1945. The radio car headed first for Brunswick for the terrible detritus of the Wolfenberg prison – torture instruments and a guillotine. A rough memorial had been put up to 550 prisoners executed there and he met a Czech and a Polish prisoner in an appalling state of malnutrition. They arrived at Celle, thirty kilometres from Belsen, on 20 April and the following day drove to the camp, five days after the first Allied troops and Richard

Dimbleby had arrived with a BBC camera crew. The conditions were even worse at Belsen because of the nightmare forced march of prisoners from camps in Poland like Auschwitz as the Russians advanced from the east. Many died on such marches or were shot when they could go no further. The Germans knew that the war would soon be over and many had abandoned the inmates of the camps to their fate. If the Allies had not arrived when they did, most would have perished. My father told us that many had been waiting for liberation and were too weak to survive – being liberated was enough. Others who had not eaten for days were given too much food by their liberators; their skeletal bodies could not process what they were given and they died too.

The terrible impact left a lasting impression on all who saw it and at first the BBC in London could not believe what was being reported and demanded confirmation from others: Dimbleby threatened to resign if the broadcast was not made. Many soldiers and journalists were so affected that they never talked about what they had seen. My father's wartime broadcasts were his finest work. He interviewed soldiers of the Oxford Yeomanry, the first troops to discover Belsen. In his fluent German he interviewed Anita and Renate Lasker. Two survivors were recorded in English, Gitta Cartanga and Helen Kulka, both from Czechoslovakia, who had both been saved from the gas chambers at Auschwitz by being sent on labour detachments.

The diary records:

> Over and over again, I was told the same story – of the parades at which people stood naked for hours and were picked out arbitrarily (allegedly incapable of work) for the gas chambers and the crematoriums, where many were burnt alive. Only a person in perfect health survived. Life and death was a question of pure chance.

That evening he recorded the first eve of Sabbath service: A group of a hundred or so in the open air, amid the corpses.

> The padre read the service in English and Hebrew. No eye was dry. Certainly not mine. Most of the celebrants were in unconcealed floods of tears.

He then gathered together the camp orchestra.

> They had got their instruments from the old camp band. Some of them played very well. They loved old jazz and played such tunes as 'I can't give you anything but love'.

My father then collected together some Russian girls and Dutch boys to sing. The Russians sang partisan songs and the Dutch a specially composed short song, 'The English, long may they live in glory'.

He also recorded a fifteen-year-old Dutch girl, Hetty Werkendamm, whose father had been half-strangled and made to shovel excreta into the 'shit pit'. In the 1990s, I published a book by Hetty, who had gone to live in Australia, called *The Children's House of Belsen*. It records her interview with my father in full. In the acknowledgements, she thanks my father and the BBC.

On his last evening at Belsen, my father was able to visit some of the Nazi guards in custody to find SS members who were prepared to talk. A doctor from Auschwitz claimed he had only been tending the sick. My father interviewed numerous prisoners and guards. He picked up a frightening cosh that the guards had used on inmates, which I keep by my bed in case of a break-in. The risk is that one blow would kill someone, which had been its purpose in the camps.

During his time at Belsen, my father realised that the rescue effort of the British medical personnel was not progressing as fast as it should. The concluding passages of his diary entry on Belsen are marked: FROM HERE ON NOT FOR PUBLICATION. These pages document the 'serious shortcomings' which delayed decisions such as the evacuation to a nearby training school, but there was no-one with the authority to do these. There was also a fear that typhoid, which was rife in the camps, would spread throughout the country.

My father, like so many, did his best. He left Belsen on 22 April and drove to the virtually flattened town of Hamm where eight out of ten of the population were living in cellars.

The Belsen broadcast went out on the evening of Sunday 27 May as *Belsen: Facts and Figures*. In late 1945, my father published with Victor Gollancz *The Lid Lifts*, based on his diaries and broadcasts. Gollancz produced an excellent little book – he was after all the publisher of *Animal Farm*. No mention of my father's criticisms or the tears of the inmates interviewed appeared in the book or the broadcast.

The German diaries are particularly powerful and exceptionally significant for the twentieth century. He believed that the concentration camp

> is one of the exclusive characteristic manifestations of our age. It is one of the distinguishing marks of the twentieth century. Never have human beings been brought so low – deliberately and with calculation brought so low … We used to turn away our eyes and shut our ears because we did not want to know: we look away now because we know too much. Because Hitler has played hell with our standards.

My father's broadcasts are still available from the BBC. They now open with the camp band playing the national anthem; there is still no mention of people being in floods of tears; and none of the criticism of the speed of help is included. His voice is very BBC received pronunciation, but it is powerful all the same. It can be accessed on the BBC website using the search terms 'Patrick Gordon Walker – Belsen Facts and Thoughts – BBC'. *The Lid Lifts* is long out of print. As it was published in 1945, with scare resources, including of paper, the first print run was necessarily small. Longer extracts from his Belsen diaries appear as an addendum at the end of this book.

FIVE

Post-War Politics

My father was back in London for the unconditional surrender of Germany and the end of the war in Europe, though he returned to Germany after VE Day. The coalition government had been in place since 1931, though there was a general election in 1935. In the war cabinet, senior Labour members of parliament held key cabinet positions, led by Clement Attlee, the deputy prime minister – this was a unique arrangement, reflecting the dire threat to Britain's survival. There had not been parliamentary elections for ten years and they were long overdue. Politics had changed dramatically since the days of Ramsay MacDonald, Stanley Baldwin and Neville Chamberlain, which seemed to belong to a different age. The war had shaken everything up, with troops fighting everywhere – and still at war against the Japanese, and women had assumed roles never thought possible.

Winston Churchill, the wartime prime minister, was determined that there should be an election, with as many troops back home as possible, and the date chosen was 5 July 1945, although the count was delayed until 25 July to allow the counting of overseas votes. The polls predicted a triumph for Churchill, in recognition of his wartime victories, but the country was in a mood for change and wanted a new leader for the post-war reconstruction. Labour under Attlee won a landslide victory, winning 393 seats to the Conservatives' 197. The Liberals were reduced to twelve seats and the National Liberals to thirty-three. The majority over the Conservatives was 196 and versus all parties was 146 seats, the first time Labour had ever had a majority in parliament. They were now planning to implement the Labour agenda for change. 'The Red Flag', the anthem of the Labour Party – though few know the words – was first sung in the House of Commons on 15 August 1945 when Clement Attlee took over as prime minister.

As my father returned to Germany after VE Day, he could not take part in any electioneering and seemed to have missed the boat. He was not in Oxford when Frank Pakenham lost to Quintin Hogg again, with Pakenham going to the Lords. His chance came, by serendipity, when the MP for Smethwick, Alf Dobbs, was killed in a car crash the day after being elected. Dobbs belonged to the boot and shoe union and my father was something altogether different, a don, Oxford educated and having attended a public school. All the same, he was chosen as the MP of a then safe Labour working-class seat. Fate was later going to rebound on him and the local party, but not for many years.

My parents had moved to a big house in Hampstead Garden Suburb, 6 Linnell Close, then a quiet backwater on the fringes of London and not as fashionable – or expensive – as it was to become. Finance must have come from Dodo, my father's mother, who had sizeable sums which she used to help her son out. She did not see why his family should suffer from his eccentric choice of career and political party. There was also a small mortgage. The Suburb was to become quite a Labour colony with Harold Wilson, Fred Willey, Frank and Elizabeth Longford and the Mandelson family, including Peter, living there. The 'posh' Labour MPs were in Hampstead proper, Douglas Jay, Frank Soskice and Roy Jenkins, and in Frognal, Hugh Gaitskell.

There was also the small matter of finally getting Judy and Carol and their cousin Andrew back from exile in Jamaica, now that it was safe to travel. This time my mother's parents, Didi and Grampie, were to accompany them home. They set off in March 1945, five days on a US troop ship to New Orleans and then a two-night train journey to New York. They sailed on the flagship of a huge ninety-two-ship convoy, part of the Ellerman Line, and the boat finally docked at Liverpool. The three returning refugees and Didi and Grampie came down by train to Euston – no mean feat then – where my mother and father were there to meet them.

After five years, no-one knew what anyone looked like, and the arrival was further confused as my parents were expecting two children, not three. My mother had also not seen her parents for over fifteen years, though they would not have changed as much as had their children. Judy was now nine, Andrew eight and Carol seven. My mother said: 'Oh there is Andrew', which did not endear her to Judy and Carol, as their mother had recognised their cousin first. They set off to their new home in Hampstead Garden Suburb, with Andrew being reunited with his parents. It must have been a trauma for all, coming from a hot country to freezing London, with parents they scarcely remembered and where they knew no-one.

The shock was even greater as on 27 February 1944, a new daughter, Ann, had been born. She as a baby had experienced the V-bombs, with their random flight path and eerie noise, which had made her nervous. The ambulance for her birth had got lost in the Blitz, now with V1 and V2 rockets making London even more vulnerable. More introductions had to be made. Gradually it became clear that my grandparents had essentially gone bust. The wartime isolation of Jamaica had played havoc with trade and agriculture, and they had not been able to keep going. They had nowhere to go but to stay with my parents – and my parents had no option but to take them in. Our grandparents still scarcely spoke to each other. It must have been a huge upheaval to all. My mother's war roles had ended and she anyway had a baby to look after and now three children in all, as well as her parents.

Reeling from all these blows, my parents had planned another new arrival to be a friend for Ann, who was much younger than her older sisters. The trouble is that two new arrivals came, Alan and Robin on 15 May 1946. Three children make an unstable alliance, where two do not, and so it proved. So, between 1944 and 1946 the family went from one child, Ann, and two parents, to five children, two parents and two grandparents – nine in all. My mother had not known she was having twins until nearly full term. We were born in a nursing home in Platts Lane,

The christening of Robin and me at the crypt of the House of Commons, July 1946. The mayor and mayoress of Smethwick were godparents. Dora, my grandmother, is in the middle and on the right are Judy, little Ann and Carol

Hampstead, with me being born fifteen minutes before Robin: I was put in a basin and Robin had the cot. Poor Ann suffered the most, torn between being with her much older sisters or linking herself with her two younger twin brothers, who anyway formed a bond together. It is no surprise that she read science when the rest of the family studied the arts. While we all stayed in the UK, she moved to America to live and bring up her family. It would not take a psychologist to work out that there was trouble ahead. Judy's equilibrium was not helped when she slipped on ice in Linnell Close Square and broke her leg. In those days it took a long time to set, but she recovered eventually.

My father was able to escape, as Parliament sat until late at night and he needed the family car. (Parliament for many years sat late to allow an MP to attend to his job (mainly his, not her) in the day – businessman, stockbroker, lawyer, barrister etc. – before going to the House. This worked better for Tory MPs than for Labour ones.) An MPs salary was £600 per annum, half what a don received. As a backbencher, my father went out to earn money from writing, but he had ambitions to play a role in the opportunity for Labour to reshape Britain and make fundamental changes to British society. Labour seemed set to be in office for a considerable time – but not for as long as they hoped. My father longed for advancement and even to scale the greasy pole to Downing Street. In October 1946, at the advanced age of thirty-nine, he became parliamentary private secretary (PPS) to Herbert Morrison, the Lord President of the Council and number two in the government, a heady rise so soon.

The self-educated Morrison liked to surround himself with middle-class intellectuals and the two of them formed a good working relationship and became friends. My father found it easy to bond with the working-class members of the Labour Party, later with the celebrated and excitable George Brown. Morrison encouraged his protégés to become really involved with the work of the government, sharing with them important papers and asking them to make policy suggestions. My father responded with proposals to reform the House of Lords, whereby its powers of delaying government business should be curtailed and life peers be appointed – from which change he was much later to benefit.

My father remained with Morrison for a year, but he was in demand. Ernest Bevin wanted him at the Foreign Office, while Morrison suggested that he should be paymaster general. In the end, he became under-secretary to Philip Noel-Baker at the Commonwealth Office. He told the prime minister, Clem Attlee, that he knew little about the Commonwealth, but that 'he would quickly acquire all that he needed to know and make good his ignorance'. He was moving quickly within the party hierarchy. The revolutionary proposals by the government were proceeding on education, the forming of the NHS and changes to unemployment pay, but it was not all plain sailing. The country had nearly bankrupted itself with debt for the war effort, particularly to the USA. Rationing continued throughout the period and there was a shortage of coal and other energy resources, leading to power cuts, which were to take the edge off the government achievements – people hoped for a future free from the privations of the war. I recall the lights going out and power shortages as a young child.

An official photograph used as a Christmas card, December 1946 of the infant twins, Alan and Robin

SIX

Family 1948 Onwards

My father, though he worked late in Parliament, had time for family life with his five children. With nine in the house including my grandparents, the house in Linnell Close, where the large Pakenham family also lived, proved too small. With financial help, I presume, from my father's mother, Dodo, and a larger mortgage, the family moved to a bigger house a few minutes away in South Square, No. 22. It was an impressive house, with seven bedrooms – the old billiard room was later divided into two to make eight. There was a small room downstairs which my grandparents could use to eat and sit, a large sitting room with double doors to another room for my father's study, a kitchen and a dining room. There were four bedrooms on the first floor, one for my parents, one for my grandparents, one for Robin and me and one for Ann, though she later moved to the top floor, so we would have a spare room for the numerous guests from Jamaica and family at home. Judy and Carol each had a room on the top floor and there was a small third room, which was to become Ann's. There was a large garden, including a redundant tennis court, and an area of grass in front of the houses in the Square where children could safely play. There were few cars then. The gas streetlights were lit each evening by the lamplighter, the milk float was powered by a horse. Delivery boys on bicycles brought some provisions, but my grandfather would set off frequently for the shops in Golders Green or Temple Fortune with his wicker shopping trolley for the large family.

There was a big church, St Jude's, a moment away, perfect for my mother and the children to attend. My mother was always a churchgoer and St Jude's was high church, which suited her perfectly. My father went to church occasionally and was

A photograph of me, aged about three to four.
Note the curls inherited from my mother

reluctant to participate in the 'handshake of peace'. When the moment came, he would fold his arms and look resolutely ahead to the embarrassment of those around him. It was reminiscent of Alan Bennett, who said there should be a part of a church where one could sit and avoid the peace. His comment was: 'We are C of E, we don't support this gesture.'

Behind the church was a large open space called Central Square, and opposite this the renowned Henrietta Barnett School. Across Central Square was a free church, into which we never went, and a Quaker meeting house. With a synagogue close by, most faiths were catered for. The suburb had been designed to have no public transport and it was a long walk to the Tube or buses in Golders Green. It was an idyllic area to grow up in for children. It was a quiet backwater close to London proper.

When we moved to South Square, Judy was twelve, Carol ten, Ann four and the twins two. Schools had to be found and the expenses met. Judy and Carol were due to go away to boarding school at eleven, but Judy reneged and won a scholarship to North London Collegiate School in Edgware. It was state aided, so there was only a small top-up fee to be paid: she could have gone free to Henrietta Barnett a couple of minutes away, but in those days, North London Collegiate was thought to be a better school. For Carol, who still did what her elder sister told her to do, it was too late to change so the next year she went to Cheltenham Ladies' College. The cost of this came from Rudolf relations in Jamaica. The families there spent little and saved up for key expenses – and education was such an essential to pay for. Otherwise, it would not have been possible. Ann was at the kindergarten of Henrietta Barnett, to which Robin and I were to follow. The school was free in those days, as it still is.

Parliamentary recesses coincided with school holidays and weekends were normally free, so we saw lots of our father at these times. My mother was pretty tied up with childcare, and she wanted to play a wider role, but women after the war were now in a box and voluntary work was the best that could be hoped for. She became involved in the nearby Wellgarth Nursery College, which trained nurses and provided childcare. Some of the nurses came from disadvantaged and single-parent families – the latter then a cause of shame – but it is now closed down. She also was actively involved with St Jude's. We obviously saw her full time, but one assumes that the adjustment from worthwhile work to voluntary activities was a difficult one. My father loved small children and I remember him being around, looking after the large garden and playing with us.

After being involved with the BBC broadcasts in the war, my father's brother, Uncle Robin, needed a job. He obviously could not return to teaching at Wellington, after resigning with the chaplain, and he rather incongruously joined the new National Coal Board at its inception. To the surprise of some, he married in 1946 the beautiful and very young Rosemary Carless, brother of Hugh Carless, who travelled with his friend Eric Newby on his *A Small Walk in the Hindu Kush*. Robin was thirty-five and had lost his hair like his brother and so many GWs, so he looked older than he was. When he was born, Robin had been what was then called a 'blue baby', which meant that there were problems with his heart – a perennial problem for male GWs. Eighteen months later, aged only thirty-seven, he went to bed and never woke up, leaving a young and pregnant widow after a year of marriage. It was a terrible tragedy for all, though I was too young to know about it at the time. Robin and Rosemary's baby, Margaret Susan, was a year younger than my brother Robin and me and we would see Rosemary and her from time to time, as they lived together near us on Haverstock Hill, between Hampstead and Swiss Cottage. Very sadly, I remember nothing about Uncle Robin, who from all accounts was charismatic and charming.

Several years after Robin died, Rosemary married the charismatic and charming Paul Rolo, a history don at Balliol College, who moved to become Professor of History at the new University of Keele in Staffordshire. They had two children together, Hugh and Jane.

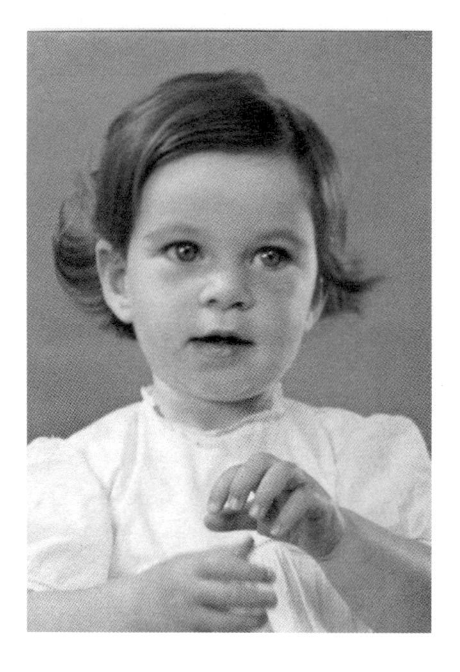

When Uncle Robin died so young, Rosemary was pregnant with Margaret Susan, who never knew her father. Here she is a few years old

SEVEN

Up the Greasy Pole: Commonwealth Secretary

After the close 1950 election result, Attlee wished to make changes to his cabinet. He was not impressed by Philip Noel-Baker, the Commonwealth secretary, to whom my father had just been appointed under-secretary – he was learning his political craft and about the Commonwealth. It was a department ideally suited to my father's knowledge of history. Noel-Baker was moved to the Ministry of Fuel to accommodate the appointment of my father, an important role with shortages of coal and energy in general. In the first five years of government, Labour had made dramatic changes to supply, nationalising coal and other utilities, but it was a time of severe shortages and rationing continued, which proved increasingly unpopular. The landslide 1945 majority of 146 was reduced in 1950 to just 6. My father was thought to have shown 'exceptional ability' and joined the cabinet after only five years in Parliament, in March 1950, as secretary of state for Commonwealth relations, a key appointment in those days. His rise had indeed been rapid.

My father was in those days a popular figure in a Labour government. The cabinet had plenty of members educated at public school and university, so he did not stand out. There were Hugh Gaitskell, Stafford Cripps, Attlee, Hugh Dalton and Sir James Chuter Ede, matched by traditional Labour trade union and working-class members: Herbert Morrison, Ernest Bevin, Aneurin Bevan and Mannie Shinwell. With such a small majority of six, time was of the essence, as there was likely to be another election soon, to aim for a working majority. Gaitskell mused that my father 'was well in with the leaders of the Labour Party' – Attlee, Bevin, Morrison and Cripps. Attlee praised my father's

The official photograph when my father joined Attlee's cabinet as secretary of state for Commonwealth relations, taken on 1 March 1950, when he was 43 years old

worth, but this had not always been reciprocated. He was a Morrison man and was influenced by his rivalry with Attlee. George Brown, then PPS to Hugh Dalton, and a future foreign secretary, joined those plotting in the Commons tearooms to replace Attlee with Bevin. It was not successful. Although my father had reservations about Attlee, who was in some ways an administrator rather than a leader, in the end he decided that he had the necessary qualities to continue leading the party.

At the Commonwealth Relations Office (CRO) there was a whole host of great challenges. The years 1945–1951 were crucial in the development of the modern Commonwealth. In 1945, the Commonwealth was an all-white club. By 1951 it was more of a multi-racial association. India and Pakistan became independent in 1947 and oversight of them passed from the India Office to the CRO. To complicate matters further the old Dominions Office and defunct Indian Office continued to exist side by side, each under its own permanent secretary – a real dog's breakfast, according to the British high commissioner in India, Sir Archibald Nye.

In January 1949, a sole permanent secretary, Percivale Liesching, was appointed but he could not get on with Philip Noel-Baker. When the reshuffle came in 1950, my father enjoyed much more harmonious relations with Liesching. There was no longer the threat of India and Pakistan leaving the Commonwealth, to which some credit should be given to my father, even though there was a risk that India's secession might take place at some stage. My father and his ministry were determined to prevent this. Careful preparations were made for the 1949 Commonwealth Prime Ministers' Conference. Travel was difficult in these days, but emissaries at a senior level were sent to visit Australia, New Zealand and South Africa. My father went to the key states, Pakistan, Ceylon and India, where he met Prime Minister Nehru three times. India would not accept allegiance to the Crown – there was too much history for this – but it was willing to accept the King as 'the symbol of the free association' of the member-states and as such, 'the head of the Commonwealth'.

It was a victory for the CRO over the Foreign Office, which wanted closer ties with all members of the Commonwealth. It was a victory for my father, as his diary proclaims. He received praise from *The Times* and *The Economist*, which saw the development as 'primarily the work of Gordon Walker'. It was a feat requiring great skill, the problem over Kashmir, which seemed for a time a danger to the whole Commonwealth, proving impossible of solution. It went to the UN and in the end war between India and Pakistan was averted. The dispute has never been fully resolved, but at least it did not destroy the Commonwealth.

In May 1950, there was severe flooding in Winnipeg, Canada, and it was felt correct that Britain should help a Commonwealth country in its hour of need, however hard it might be to find the funds. My father announced in the House of Commons on 25 May that an aeroplane had been chartered to 'carry about eight

In 1950 there was severe flooding in Manitoba in Canada, and as Commonwealth relations secretary, my father had a photoshoot of a plane taking supplies from the UK. We were 4 and I can just remember that Robin and I were rather keen on the soft toys that were going in the plane, rather than, as we hoped, to us

tons of sheets and pillowcases, towels, curtain material, hospital and children's blankets, Elastoplast dressings, and some toys for the younger children'. Robin and I were just four at the time, and I do not remember it, but we went with our father to see the plane fly off. There were press photographs at the airport in the UK from which the supplies were being sent of us two with my father seeing off the plane. We are all dressed smartly, with matching coats, and the box with the toys was on the tarmac for the press photographs. Robin and I each desperately wanted a teddy bear and were bereft when we were told we could just hold them before they went onto the plane.

My father impressed many at the CRO, receiving praise for his achievements, but one issue was irrevocably to harm his reputation. This was the exile of Seretse Khama, which the *New Statesman* suggested showed 'Britain's support for the colour bar, opposition to mixed marriages and sympathy with South African racial policy'. It was not as extreme as that. Seretse Khama was the heir to the chieftainship of the Bamangwato tribe in Bechuanaland (modern Botswana). His uncle, Tshekedi, acted as regent while he gained a legal training in London. Before completing his studies Seretse married an Englishwoman, Ruth Williams. The British government tried to get him to renounce his chieftainship, but when he refused, my father announced that he would be exiled from home for five years.

There was a storm of criticism, from Labour and the Conservatives. The press universally disapproved and in Parliament seven Labour MPs voted with the opposition. It was a clear-cut moral scandal, and my father was the villain of the piece. His role was to support what had been a cabinet decision and he had inherited the problem from his predecessor, Noel-Baker. There are several reasons why Whitehall objected to the marriage. Firstly, it was resented by the Bamangwato tribe. Seretse did not tell Tshekedi until just before his marriage, as he knew he and the tribe would disapprove. There were tribal meetings (*kgotlas*) in Bechuanaland. The first two sided with Tshedki, the third with Seretse.

Left to itself, Britain might have supported Seretse, but there was the major hurdle of the opposition from the government of South Africa, where in 1949 the Prohibition of Mixed Marriages Act had been passed. If Seretse was allowed to return, there was the threat that South Africa could lay claim to the High Commission Territories, of Basutoland, Bechuanaland and Swaziland, creating a constitutional crisis for the Commonwealth and stirring up opposition from the white settlers of Southern Rhodesia and Kenya. It might be best, for the greater good, to leave Seretse in exile.

Noel-Baker had failed to secure Seretse's agreement, and it fell to my father to try again. He proposed that Seretse should accept a five-year postponement, in which time Tshekedi would also be outlawed. My father had gone against some advice with his proposal, but Seretse refused and leaked details of the suggested course, with my father taking the brunt of the criticism. Nor has he had a good press from historians, but there was no easy way to please all, and the threat of opposition from South Africa, starting on the route to apartheid, was genuine. My father spelt out the intractable problem for cabinet:

> Our major concern, in the African inhabitants of the three Territories, is to preserve the territories from the [South African] union: this is even more important than the case of Seretse.

The Seretse matter involved complex, not simple issues and my father has been seen to be on the wrong side of the issue, supporting his exile. Perhaps it is best summed up in his words:

> Five years ago, the overwhelming evidence [was] that if a British government, by installing Seretse as chief, put its official seal upon a mixed marriage in the midst of South African territory, there would be such a wave of insensate rage that co-operation would be withdrawn and we would lose the three Territories.

My father seems to have seen Seretse and Ruth Khama as troublemakers who had to be sacrificed on geopolitical grounds and paid little heed to their point of view. The incoming Conservative government was even more ruthless and decisive. Seretse was told that he was permanently removed from the chieftainship. He returned in 1956 as a private citizen with Ruth at his side and became the first president of an independent Botswana, which remained out of the control of South Africa and has thrived as an independent state. That at least is on the plus side.

My father was a keen cricketer, at school and Oxford and for the BBC Bush House team, the Bushmen. Here he seems to be sharing cricket with some electioneering

My father's time as Commonwealth secretary attracted criticism, particularly with the intractable Seretse problem, but it was competent and creditable, nonetheless. He was an important figure in Attlee's second administration, which was a poor successor to the first. Some ministers had served since 1940 in the wartime coalition and the Korean War cast its shadow. Cripps and Bevin were ill and to stand down. Attlee's health too was poor, Morrison was not a strong foreign secretary, and Bevan and Harold Wilson resigned over health service charges and increasing arms expenditure. After six years of major social change, against a background of continued hardships from the war, the Labour government had run out of steam.

My father was against going to the country in 1951, with good reason, describing it as a major error of judgement. The 1951 election saw a majority of votes cast for Labour, but a Conservative government gained a working majority of seventeen seats. Churchill was back. The decision to go the country was to lead to thirteen years of Tory rule.

EIGHT

In Opposition

While my father had been a minister and in the cabinet, his job was full time: days in the ministry and evenings in the House of Commons, and travel – to India and Pakistan over Kashmir and to South Africa in March 1951. When he was a junior minister in the CRO, he went with my mother to Australia, New Zealand and Canada in 1948 and 1949. The general election loss in October 1951 meant that, no longer being a minister, his salary was suddenly cut and money was tight again, though he did stay on the opposition front bench, for which there was a small remuneration in those days. On the plus side, there was more time to see the family. By 1951, Judy was fifteen, at school at North London Collegiate, and Carol was thirteen and away at Cheltenham Ladies' College, the first one to go away to school. Then the age gap to Ann, 7, and the twins, 5. Ann was at the Henrietta Barnett School, two minutes from our house, and Robin and I were in the kindergarten of the school, which took boys in the first two years of what was then an exclusively girls' school. Our classroom was essentially set up for girls and I recall on the first day telling Robin that we should not play with the dolls' house. How times have changed – our grandsons are very happy to play with our dolls' house, and toys are no longer seen as his or hers, a great improvement.

Our house in the Garden Suburb fitted us all in: Judy, Carol and Ann on the top floor, and Robin and I always shared a large room that later became our father's study. My grandparents had a small room, which just took two single beds. As they were scarcely speaking it must have been an ordeal. We had a small television in the corner of the dining room. In those days, there was one hour of children's programmes and then a break

POLLING DAY, 23rd FEBRUARY 7 a.m.—9 p.m.

POLL CARDS

1. Political Parties may no longer, by law, send out Poll Cards.

It is now the duty of the Returning Officer to send you an official Poll Card, which will tell you your Polling Station and your number on the electoral roll.

It is useful, but not at all necessary, to take this Card with you when you vote.

BALLOT PAPER

2. If you wish to vote LABOUR you should put your X against the name of GORDON WALKER, like this :—

P. C. GORDON WALKER	X

AFTER THE VOTE

3. It will help the Labour Party very much if you will give your name and address (and, if you remember it, your electoral number) to the Labour representative outside your Polling Station. Best of all give him your Poll Card.

Printed by Cape Hill Press Ltd., Hume St., Smethwick and Published by Alderman Mrs. E. M. Farley, Co-op Rooms, 383-391, High St., Smethwick.

During the campaign I have done my best to put my policy—the policy of the Labour Party—before you.

I am convinced that if a Conservative Government were returned three things would go up :— unemployment, prices, Communism. That has been the experience of every country with a Conservative Government since the war.

Another Labour Government will mean that social security is secure ; that we keep full employment ; that our magnificent record of industrial peace will continue ; that a concerted onslaught is made on the cost of living.

Labour puts the nation first. Labour stands for the workers and all the useful people.

So, FORWARD SMETHWICK with LABOUR.

P. C. Gordon Walker

Every mother is naturally proud of her children. I am very proud of my five ; but it's a big job rearing a family.

I don't know where we mothers would be without a Government that really does put the family first.

LABOUR has helped the mothers of Britain to bring up the bonniest babies and children in the world by the new Health Service (which the Conservatives voted against), free provision of orange juice, cod liver oil, milk at Schools and in a dozen other ways.

Let us be proud of our children but let us also be proud of our Labour Government.

Audrey Gordon Walker

A family photograph used as an election card for the 1951 election, which Labour lost. It is taken in the garden of our house in Hampstead Garden Suburb

in transmission, so that children could do their homework or have their tea. When my father was working or writing in his study, we were forbidden from making a noise and were sent into the garden to play. It was a really large garden with terraces, a circular lawn surrounded by flower beds, and a shrubbery leading to the abandoned tennis court, which later became a croquet lawn when my father gave up tennis.

After the war we kept chickens for a time, despite the foxes. Judy and Carol used to tend them and feed them and count that all were safe. One day, we had a rare treat of roast chicken for lunch. My older sisters were suspicious and went down to the coop, to find that two chickens were missing. They removed them from the table and ceremoniously buried them, depriving all of us of our special meal. We sometimes were sent a box of oranges from relations in South Africa and at the end of the war distant friends sent a sheep from New Zealand. My mother took it to the butcher in Golders Green, who was very suspicious, assuming it was from the black market. Eventually it was butchered and made several splendid meals.

The Suburb had been designed to have houses of all sizes and as an escape from London. Most of the squares – South, North and Central, Linnell Close and so on – had areas of grass in front of them where children could safely play. There were very few cars then, normally only those belonging to the residents, not all of whom had cars. Where we were, all the houses were large and with families. There were lots of children born between 1945 and 1948, the famous post-war bulge, now the baby-boomers.

My parents had ready friends from Oxford days, the Longfords/Pakenhams, and added the Collinses – Norman Collins was a novelist and television executive who left the BBC and was instrumental, with Lew Grade, in setting up ATV, part of ITV, which broke the BBC monopoly and funded itself with advertisements. There were political friends too, who came to the house, and the local Labour Party had its garden party in our garden, where we all helped as we could. There were Douglas and Peggy Jay, with their beautiful twin daughters Helen and Catherine, Roy Jenkins, Dick Taverne and others. Harold Wilson lived a couple of streets away, but we did not seem to mix with his family much, or the Willeys, who lived in North Square, where the houses were smaller than in South Square.

The Suburb had no transport in those days – there are now hoppa buses – so it was a twenty-minute walk to the Underground, buses and shops. We had bicycles, but the three youngest were not allowed to go far. Grampie, after he had raked and restoked the coal boiler, would go down to the shops with his shopping trolley, while Didi looked after the children. My father was busy, and my mother used to accompany him to events and sometimes abroad, so we were often in the care of our grandparents. My mother was helped by Eileen, the nurse who had accompanied the trio on the wartime trip to Jamaica, whose fireman husband did odd jobs in his time off. It was always fun to see if there was anything we could do to help. It was a long way to North London Collegiate in Edgware for Judy and then for Ann when she went too. Twenty minutes' walk to Golders Green (unless someone gave them a lift), down what my father referred to as 'Dead Man's Gulch' between Golders Green crematorium on one side and the cemetery on the other. Then six stops on the Northern line and then a walk up the drive to the school. Judy was ten years older than Robin and me and Carol eight, so we did not see much of them and they would both go away to Oxford University when we were eight or nine.

The Hampstead Heath extension was ten minutes or so away from us. The playing fields had been turned over to allotments in the war – they were still allotments when we went for walks – and further north, there were the remains of Nissen huts and gun placements, from when there had been wartime anti-aircraft batteries. It was roped off, but it was fun to play there

A studio portrait of the five children, Judy, Carol, Ann, Alan and Robin, on the table in the dining room at 22 South Square, around 1950/1. In almost all such photos, I am with Judy, Robin with Carol and Ann in the middle

and imagine the war. There is a long gap between Golders Green and Hampstead stations on the Underground and the plan originally was to have a Tube stop in the Suburb, near these wartime allotments. This had never been used, but it was opened up in the war as an air raid shelter and there was hope that it would be fully used, which would have kept the Suburb more attached to other centres. But it was not to be, as the Suburb luminaries thought it would have harmed the ambience and peace as designed by the founders. It would have made a huge difference for teenagers and older children living in the semi-rural idyll. For young children and young teenagers the Suburb was perfect, but less so as one grew up.

My father now had recesses as a backbencher, so he could spend more time with us. He was good company, though the loss of his minister's salary meant that he had to return to writing to earn money. He was working on a book which became *Restatement of Liberty*, a philosophical discussion of Locke and Mill and an attack on Cartesian dualism. Its scope was wide, covering Calvin as well as Descartes. Few active politicians could have written such a book and maybe few could have read it. Although I studied philosophy, it is the only one of his books that I have not read in full.

My father with Ann, Robin and me, showing his friendly, family side

NINE

The Commonwealth Revisited and the Divided Labour Party

My father extended his experience from the Commonwealth Relations Office to become Labour's leading expert on the subject. He wrote an article, 'Policy for the Commonwealth', for a Fabian collection of essays. He believed in the Commonwealth as an interchange of people as well as governments. His imagination had been fired by extensive tours, going to India in 1948 over Kashmir, and in July and August 1949, as under-secretary before becoming the minister, he had travelled 41,000 miles, visiting New Zealand, Australia and Canada before moving to the colonies in central Africa – my mother accompanied him to Australia and New Zealand, leaving her parents to look after the children.

His book *The Commonwealth* was published in 1962, increasing his credentials. The Commonwealth was still very white then and my father became out of step with Labour policy on central Africa. He believed that bulwarks should be set up against South African encroachment. He was at odds with many of his colleagues and the Commonwealth was fraught with difficulties for politicians of all parties. As a historian he took the long view, decades, centuries, whereas politicians know that a week is a long time. His aim at partnership was to him the antithesis of apartheid, though it may have not been clear when he wrote that partnership was

> to build societies in Africa in which the children and grandchildren of whites can live in peace and prosperity with their more numerous neighbours of other races in Africa. No policy that does not look three or four generations ahead can be anything but a mirage in Africa.

It was to take forty years to see the end of the policy of apartheid. My father seemed to believe that it was the duty of the white settlers to raise standards. He was no racist and racism was anathema to him. In *An Outline of Man's History*, he had stressed that 'there is no evidence that any race is superior to any other'. But he was not sensitive to the Africans, and the partnership concept was used by the settlers in Northern and Southern Rhodesia as an effective disguise for white supremacy. The federation issue did harm to my father and the Commonwealth, however intractable, was seldom at the core of British politics. He wanted the Labour Party to put the Commonwealth at its heart, but it was not a vote winner with the party or the public. When Commonwealth issues hit the headlines, like immigration from the West Indies or Asia, my father's pro-Commonwealth stance was unpopular. This, and the fact that his wife was from Commonwealth Jamaica, were to coalesce disastrously in Smethwick. In opposition, it was difficult to keep the party factions together, as has been the case in recent years. Any political party is an amalgam of differing factions, which can create more heat and less light and run deeper than fighting the other party. (The Church is often similar.) There was a rift between Bevan and Gaitskell, in simple terms left and right. In 1951 Bevan resigned as minister of labour and a group of Bevanites was formed. Attlee, still prime minister, demanded the end of a party within a party – as was Momentum under Jeremy Corbyn – and Gaitskell rallied the right of the party, which was where my father now stood. The next issue was German rearmament, about which my father felt vehemently and he tried to rally support for training German troops in Wales, against which Welsh Labour MP Leo Abse objected most strongly.

By 1954, the Conservatives were doing badly, and Labour could have struck a blow if they had remained united, but Bevan openly challenged Attlee, who stayed on as leader of the opposition. There had been factional fighting within the party before, and maybe Attlee should have gone sooner and allowed someone else to try to unite the party – but it would have still been a difficult task. Bevan, having been made minister of labour in 1951, finally resigned; as Attlee commented, 'our outside left has shot through his own goal'. Harold Wilson replaced him. The opportunity had been lost.

In 1955 Winston Churchill announced his resignation as prime minister: he had been in power since 1940 except for 1945–1951 and it was time for a new leader. Conservative leaders 'emerged' then, rather than be elected, and Anthony Eden took over and immediately called a general election. The Conservatives easily won, despite an unimpressive manifesto, with a clear majority. My father's majority in Smethwick fell from 9,726 to 6,495.

TEN

22 South Square: 1951–1955

Defeat in 1955 had had a sobering effect on Labour, who feared that they would be in opposition for a long time. I remember one occasion when my father came back much earlier than normal, before having a brief sleep at home. He explained that Labour MPs were to return later that night, in the hope of catching out the Conservatives, who might have gone home and not returned. The ruse did not work, as the Conservatives used to stay on in the bars, so they were still present and did not lose a vote.

In 1951, Judy was fifteen and Carol was thirteen, Ann seven and the twins five. Family holidays initially consisted of my parents and the three girls going off by car; Robin and I could not fit in the family car as well, though earlier there is a photo of all five children in the back seat, with the twins sitting on the arm rests – there were of course no seat belts in those days. The five – without the twins – would set off sometimes to France as financial controls on what money one could take on holiday began to ease a bit. Holidays were simple and enjoyable for those who went. The twins were left at home with our grandparents, which suited us as we had more freedom when our mother was away.

In those days MPs did not go to their constituency nearly as often as now. There were no second constituency homes, few expenses to fiddle, no swopping of homes for tax reasons – and no pensions as MPs were deemed to be self-employed, so should make their own provisions. My father went to Smethwick maybe once a month and stayed with his constituency agent, sometimes accompanied by my mother. The children went occasionally and stayed with our mother in a B&B. On several occasions, when we were older, we were taken to watch West Bromwich Albion, half of whose ground was in Smethwick and half in

West Bromwich, in the directors' box. This was always a special treat and I have always supported West Bromwich and still do, though I only see them play in London against Crystal Palace – fervently supported by my brother Robin and his family – when they are in the same division. WBA is one of those yo-yo teams that regularly go up and down. In London, when Robin and I were at day prep school, pupils tended to support Spurs if they lived in north London and Fulham in the south: Arsenal and Chelsea were not major teams then.

One benefit of Labour remaining in opposition was that my father had more time with his family (see also Chapter 8). We were always short of money and my father had to write articles and do broadcasts, sometimes for German TV, where it was rare to find a British politician so fluent in German. In those days there was still not a lot of money around for anybody, but the beginning of the consumer boom had finally begun, after the deprivations of war, leading to Harold Macmillan's 'never had it so good' slogan. We seemed to be poor in comparison and school fees for five children had to be met, though not at the level of today. Judy had achieved her scholarship to North London Collegiate School, Carol's Cheltenham fees continued to be paid for by relations in Jamaica and day school fees were manageable in those days. We did not feel deprived, because at our age, we did not relate riches to happiness, and the consumer boom was only just under way. The family never spent money readily; none of us have really felt comfortable with taxis, for example. The only time we had smart presents was when Judy later married someone with money – and very welcome they were too.

Each anniversary, my father splashed out, untypically, and gave my mother a household gadget which was ahead of its time, expensive and often more trouble than it was worth and unreliable. There was a potato peeler in a drum, where one rotated the top with a handle – it never really worked – and was no better than peeling them by hand, a vacuum cleaner that

The whole family in the sitting room of 22 South Square. Note the stylish furniture and the lack of carpet

certainly was not a Dyson and finally a washing-up machine. The dishwasher was a boon, even though you had to rinse everything before putting it in – I still do this, to the annoyance of my family. It saved us from a rota of washing up, drying and putting away. My brother Robin worked out that if he broke a plate on the first day of the school holidays, he was banned from the kitchen for the duration. One of the gifts was an automatic carving knife, so my mother must have been carving the joint for once. The knife had not been put in properly and she tried to catch it, while it was still rotating. There was a lot of blood.

Sunday lunch was when the family all met together whenever possible – my parents, five children, my grandparents and sometimes Father Masters, the vicar of St Jude's. On one occasion the verger came too, and my father invited the Roman Catholic priest and his 'housekeeper' to stir things up. My father was musing on the origin of the word 'verger'. He went to his study and got the vast *Oxford English Dictionary* down and looked up the word. He returned to the dining room, and read out: 'verger – rod, staff, penis'. The poor man went purple with embarrassment, and we did not know where to look – he did not come again. My mother of course did the cooking and my father normally carved, except the once as above. When there were no guests, my father would set the family a topic for conversation, the Dissolution of the Monasteries or some subject one of us was studying at school. Everyone would talk at once, carrying out concurrent conversations across the table – bedlam. The youngest were overpowered and when we complained my father would say: 'Drop your words of wisdom into a pool of silence.' We protested that there never was such a pool and so we started to talk over someone and interrupt to say something. This is an annoying habit which I have not been able totally to overcome.

In 1955, Judy was nineteen and was on her way to Oxford and Lady Margaret Hall, to which Carol, now seventeen, would follow her from Cheltenham Ladies. In those days there were no mixed colleges. Ann was eleven and off to follow Judy to North London Collegiate. Robin and I were nine and moved to attend Arnold House preparatory school in St John's Wood, where my cousin Andrew had been before going to Stowe. We were driven to Golders Green and then took the bus to school. Our uniform was red with green piping – however loud this was, we knew we were superior to The Hall school, which had pink blazers. It was quite safe for children to travel to school in uniform then, even if not always so now. We were deemed to be under school discipline whenever we were in uniform, and woe betide if you did not raise your cap to adults or give up your seat on the bus – they would report any infringement back to the headmaster. It was quite a small school and we made good friends there and I recall it as a happy place where we were adequately taught.

Its location meant that there were many Jewish pupils – Jonathan Miller was the most famous old boy – and from the Suburb too. No distinctions were ever made and a rota of parents to take us to Golders Green bus station was organised. The children taken by car were our friends: Robert Harbermann, whom I have kept up with, Roderick Collins, son of Norman Collins and brother of Ann's friend Cordy, and others. Robin and I seemed to be about the only boys who did not have a bar mitzvah and so did not receive the usual gifts on these occasions. We went home one day to say we had a new friend called Ari and were told to call him, more properly, Harry. In fact, he was Greek, and his name was short for Aristophanes. The sports ground was far away at Canons Park on what is now the Jubilee line, one stop before Stanmore. In the summer we sometimes played cricket on the Heath extension and Robin and I could walk home through the old Nissen huts and allotments. St John's Wood had been badly bombed and sometimes we were able to get onto the undeveloped land later made into luxury homes. There was a synagogue right by the school and at some stage, after we had left, the school sold off some of the small playground for an extension and parking for the synagogue. The school is still flourishing.

Children were allowed much more freedom than now, and everyone had a bicycle. From a young age we could set off with some biscuits and a bottle of Tizer. When we were a bit older Robin and I could cycle to Temple Fortune, which had a toy shop where we could spend our small amount of pocket money. We increased our circle of friends in the Suburb and set off to the Lyttelton Playing Fields where we could cycle along the river. Games of rounders and cricket were arranged on the oases of grass in every square. Having a twin brother meant there was always a playmate, so we were self-sufficient. Robin was cleverer than me and I had to have extra tuition to keep abreast. My father and brother had photographic memories, but Judy was the academic star.

About this time, we acquired a Jack Russell terrier called Tim, who only obeyed my father. We took him for walks and when

The five children in the garden of 22 South Square, which looks staged, in 1952. The fierce dog at the front was Tim, who nipped children's fingers

he reached the kerb – there were few cars – my father tapped his walking stick twice and Tim stopped. One more tap and he set off again. He used to nip any children in the street who came up to pat him – he would be put down in five minutes now. He lived in a basket under the kitchen table and growled and bared his teeth to anyone coming in the back door. When we returned from school – Ann, Robin and me – the front door was locked, but the back door was left open in those days. I was the only one to brave going past Tim and then I opened the front door for the others to come in. He roamed across the Suburb, crossing at zebra crossings in search of a mate; he often ended up at the police station, when someone assumed he was lost, and there was a fee of ten shillings to pay – quite a sum then. Once he disappeared for several months but we kept seeing him with a particular woman. We had to go to the police station with the woman, who was convinced that Tim was hers. She called out to Tim, but he gave little response. My father had taken his stick and tapped it twice and Tim came to him immediately, so the police decided he was our dog and we were reunited with him. The poor woman was bereft.

Robin and I of course each had godparents, having been christened in the crypt in the House of Commons. The mayor of Smethwick was my godfather, along with my mother's brother, Neville, while the lady mayoress was Robin's godmother. My godmother was Lisa Sainsbury, whose husband Bob was one of the partners of what were then shops, supermarkets now. I was always told that Lisa had been a girlfriend of my father, and she was certainly extremely generous. She was a van den Bergh, whose family created margarine, so she was incredibly rich in her own right, probably more than Bob. She gave me £5 for Christmas and birthday, which was a lot of money when I was young, but unfortunately, she did not allow for inflation and the cheques never increased in value. They lived in an amazing house in Smith Square in Westminster and were great patrons of the arts – they financed the Sainsbury wing at the National Gallery. (Bob's brother Alan helped build the Clore Gallery, the Tate extension.) At their house they had paintings and sculptures by the very best artists. We used to go to birthday parties there, as her children were about the same age as the three youngest GWs. The sitting room was on the first floor and at the foot of the steps up was a Henry Moore statue. Robin, who was always nervous, whispered to me: 'Does it bite?'

When in a couple of years, it was being decided where Robin and I would go to school after Arnold House, Lisa Sainsbury came to the rescue. My parents could not have afforded boarding school and looked around for who might help. My paternal grandmother could help, but not with the fees for two boys. My mother shared the worry with Lisa, who exclaimed that for every pound they earned, or had from unearned income, above a certain threshold, she and Bob were paying 2s. 6d. extra, so they were in fact losing money rather than gaining it. In those days, the cost of education could be set against tax, which pleased her. She offered to pay my fees, which would effectively cost her sixpence in the pound but be worth the full amount to my parents. My mother explained that it was not fair that I benefited and not Robin, so she agreed to pay for him too. In all, she helped eleven godchildren and children of friends with such school fees. For good or bad, we were to be sent away at thirteen, having, unusually at the time, been at a day prep school.

We had holidays, either towing a caravan to stay on friends' land or renting one in the West Country. Our car was not really powerful enough for towing and there was one famous occasion

The family on holiday with a caravan. My father is passing a kettle to me and Robin is behind with a milk pail. Judy is waiting to pass a basket to my father. My mother and Ann are looking on and Carol is at the back, with another basket. We also had a tent for Judy and Carol

when we started to go backwards on a hill and had to be rescued by the RAC. There were tents for my older sisters, who would come by train, and the rest of us would crowd into the small caravan. One evening, Judy and Carol and my parents went out, leaving the three younger children alone. Robin was irate and threw his socks out of the window where the next morning it was discovered that they had been eaten by a cow: it became a phrase to be repeated in the family. We once stayed in a simple pub at Piddletrenthide. We got a rubber tyre blown up and swam at Weymouth and milked the cows at a nearby farm. The best bit was that at breakfast, my father and the two boys were given two boiled eggs but my mother and the three girls had only one. You could have heard their screams of disapproval in nearby Alton Pancras.

In our last two years at Arnold House, we had Saturday morning school in preparation for the Common Entrance exam. It was from nine o'clock to eleven, and afterwards we would go with a group of friends on the bus to the nearby Lord's Cricket Ground with a packed lunch, where we would watch Middlesex in county cricket. At Test matches, we queued all around the ground and children were allowed to sit on the grass. Thus started a life-long fascination with the game.

ELEVEN

In Opposition 1955–1963

With the Conservatives having chosen a new leader, Anthony Eden, it was time for Labour to follow suit. Clem Attlee had become leader of the opposition in 1935 and was then deputy prime minister from 1940 to 1945, prime minister from 1945 to 1951 and again leader of the opposition from 1951 to 1955. He had therefore been deputy prime minister, prime minister or leader of the opposition for twenty years, an unprecedented length of service. Replacing such a leader was not to be an easy task – there had been much jockeying for the throne while he stayed on.

An election for the new leader was announced and my father switched allegiance from Herbert Morrison to Hugh Gaitskell, who represented the wing of the party most compatible with my father's beliefs. Morrison was sixty-seven and seemed to be losing his powers and Gaitskell had the most chance of taking on Nye Bevan. My father saw Gaitskell as the future and his battle with Bevan was of great importance, for it would decide whether Labour was to be a party of power or of protest – a debate which was to dog the party through the Blair years to Jeremy Corbyn.

In December 1955, Gaitskell had a resounding victory over Bevan, with Morrison a distant third, and he went on to be shadow prime minister, which suited my father and his wing of the party. It was still necessary to try to unite the party and Bevan became shadow foreign secretary, as a first stage. Bevan had always been at odds with my father. My father was an intellectual, well read and knowledgeable about the world and politics, but lacked skills in public speaking. Bevan was a self-made man, and his strength and support was in his oratory.

As my father wrote in his obituary of Bevan: 'He thought with his tongue. His sense of superiority made him a compulsive talker. But the abuse that came off his tongue identified himself with ways to defeat the Conservatives as well as his colleagues.'

The general election defeat in 1955 had led to a post-mortem of what Labour had hoped would be a victory. An enquiry into the cause of the problem was led by Harold Wilson, which reported that Labour, in the realms of organisation, was still in the 'penny-farthing stage' and our 'machine is rusty and deteriorating with age'. This was scarcely surprising as Labour had only ever been in office for six years and, in that period, there was much to be done and achieved in social change and nationalisation, rather than worrying about the party operation. At the 1955 party conference, the traditionalists did not support Wilson's report. Bevan decided that there was no virtue in greater speed, if the 'vehicle was heading for a precipice'.

Despite party dissensions, Labour was given a fillip by Anthony Eden's invasion of Egypt and the Suez Canal following Gamal Abdel Nasser's seizing control of the crucial sea thoroughfare and nationalising it. Hitherto it had mainly been owned by British and French shareholders. Israel invaded Sinai and Britain and France issued a resolution for a ceasefire, which was ignored. British and French paratroopers landed along the canal. Nasser sank ships and blocked the canal, and the USA, the USSR, the UN and public opinion were all strongly against the invasion. The canal was blocked for six months, and Britain and France were shown to have lost their influence in the world. Eden, who was not well, resigned and Harold Macmillan emerged as the new leader, another old Etonian.

At this stage, with a charismatic leader in Gaitskell, Labour felt they should be heading to victory in the next election. Macmillan felt that the Conservative Party might only last in power for a matter of months, but despite his remote bearing, he proved masterly at public relations. Britain could finally begin to escape from austerity; houses were built and rationing was in the past. His slogan 'You've never had it so good' typified the new emphasis on consumerism and proved to be a vote winner. In the October 1959 election, the Tories saw their majority rise to 100 seats. A record three elections had been won in a row, and Labour still had a long way to go to prove that they were electable.

TWELVE

The Suburb: 1955–1959

By 1955, the family was growing up. There were tensions between my mother and her parents, Didi and Grampie, who were still living with us, especially Didi, who was always right and was not afraid to make this clear. My father sailed serenely on, locked away in his study, except when playing tennis. My cousin Andrew Rudolf told me that the strain on my mother led to a stomach ulcer, and she always had digestion problems thereafter.

Before Carol went to Oxford, she spent the summer working in a hotel in Brittany and my parents, Ann and the twins set off on holiday to visit her. We had not made any reservations, even though it was high season. As we arrived at each place on the way, my father would go to the tourist office to find out where we could stay the night. The rest of us sat quietly in the car awaiting his return; you could see from the look on his face whether he had been successful. We stayed in some strange places, one of which was a grand hotel where US troops had been billeted in the war and which had never recovered. Robin and I always had to share a room and bed and we used to put the bolster down the middle. Poor Ann, always nervous, had a room of her own and often sought solace with our parents.

When the twins were excluded from family holidays, aged around eleven, we were sent off to quasi-religious boys' camps – only boys – normally recommended by Cousin Andrew, who was a devout Christian. Scandals have since affected camps like this, led by the ordained Fletcher brothers, David and Jonathan, and John Smyth, who liked beating boys, which most of those who attended were used to at school. The first one we went to was in north Wales, an idyllic setting. As long as we attended morning and evening prayers and talks, we could set off to the beach to swim.

There was no misbehaviour by the staff that we saw, though it was wise not to sit in the back of the coach with the director of the camps. The only women had a separate row of bell tents and were known as 'lady helpers' – women are always kept in their place by evangelicals. Cousin Andrew was one of the team and subsequently married one of these helpers, Juliet Pritchett. They had a happy and Christian family and three children – Sophie, Jessica and Christian. Another camp in the Lake District was less successful and fraught with problems and misbehaviour.

I was perhaps the most adventurous of the family. I had riding lessons on Hampstead Heath and later went on a ski trip on my own with the Ski School of Great Britain. Robin was always more nervous and cerebral and was cleverer than me. His memory helped him to flourish. We played versions of cricket designed for two and a game called 'through-threw', played with a tennis ball and created by my father, which he taught to us. You scored one point if an opponent dropped the ball after it had bounced and two points if it went through the opponent's legs. We taught it to our children, and they will teach it to their children. Robin was an expert, but nobody dared beat my father. There were tennis courts at the side of the garden belonging to the Henrietta Barnett School which we could use at weekends. When I finally beat my father by mistake, he immediately gave up tennis and took up croquet – I knew by now to ensure I lost, which was not difficult.

With Judy and Carol off to Oxford, there was room for people to stay. Tom Meade, the son of James Meade, who had been a brilliant economist helping the Labour government, before becoming head of a Cambridge college, was one who stayed while training to be a doctor and there were others. My mother, who had found coming to Oxford from Jamaica a frightening time, always gave a warm welcome to anyone who came to London from Jamaica, especially from Hampton School. Some came to stay and she regularly held reunion parties in our garden, including her old teacher, Miss Agnes Campbell. These were jolly occasions.

Ann was still at North London Collegiate School and Robin and I were at Arnold House. We were very distant in age from Judy and Carol, at a time when the age gap was important. With both of them at Oxford, we scarcely saw them. There were scores more male colleges than women's ones, as was still the case when I went there, but not now. Their boyfriends used to come and stay, in separate rooms of course, and they were not interested in the three younger siblings. Girls used to get married much younger in those days than we did, and considerably younger than our children. Judy was squired by Graham Carleton Greene at Oxford onwards. He was the son of Hugh Carleton Greene, whom my father and uncle had worked for during the war in the BBC's German service; Hugh would go on to be a liberal and reforming director general of the BBC in the 1960s, having stayed with the Corporation since the war. Judy and Graham were married in 1957.

Carol had taken up in Oxford with a South African called David Brierley, who came to stay when Carol returned home, for, I think, quite a while, though I was away at school most of the time. Carol told me that David came into the sitting room once when my father was reading, as was his normal habit when there were visitors. My father looked up from his book and said: 'You seem to be here rather a lot, young man, why don't you come and stay?' He did not mean this rudely, it was more absent-mindedness. David did not take kindly to this remark, which was not surprising and he felt it might be best if he went and lodged nearby with friends of the family. It did not affect David and Carol's relationship and they were married in 1960.

By 1959, Ann was at senior school aged fifteen, and at thirteen, through the generosity of Lisa Sainsbury, my godmother, Robin and I were off in the October to Wellington College. When asked if we wanted to be together in the Hardinge, the house where our father and uncle Robin had been so successful, a mistake which more alert parents would have avoided, we said yes. As always before, we were again to be collectively known as the twins.

Robin and me at Wellington, in 1963.
We were not as successful as our father and uncle.

It was a rude shock. Times had improved from when my father was there, but not by a huge amount. There was still fagging, beatings and occasional homosexuality and an emphasis on physical strength over academic prowess. Almost everyone else there had been at boarding prep school and it was explained to us that it was rather like going to prison without having been in borstal first.

Matters were not helped by the fact that we were split for the first couple of terms when being together would have been helpful. Whereas we should both have gone into a holding house for a couple of terms, Robin did so, but being the older twin, I went straight into the main house, tough as it was, with an immediate introduction to fagging and house spirit. When Robin moved into the Hardinge proper, it was too late and by then we had found our feet; we thereafter got in each other's way.

My first term was marred when the school had a mock election for the October 1959 general election. The head of school was the Conservative candidate and the head of rugby stood for the

Liberals. Something came over me to put myself forward as the Labour candidate – there had never been one before. I persuaded Robin to be my agent, but he was nobbled and withdrew, and I was on my own. I recall getting votes from a few sympathisers – I am not sure that it was a secret ballot – but I was a marked man from then onwards, given all the worst chores, having to do cross-country running and subsequently being beaten by the victorious Conservative candidate. It set me on a path to be a rebel.

When we were at Wellington, my father bemoaned that he had never been offered a governorship at the school. My brother and I explained that, as it was then Labour policy to abolish private schools – a course further enhanced when he was secretary of state for education, when he had to take personal responsibility for such a policy – it was hardly surprising that they felt that they could overlook even such a distinguished old Wellingtonian. It showed the dichotomy he faced from the combination of his conservative upbringing and his left-wing beliefs.

At South Square, to which we returned in school holidays, there were frequent family visitors, including Andrew Rudolf, who had been with Judy and Carol in Jamaica and then with them at Oxford. He was an only child and his parents lived in a flat without a garden. He took over a section of the old tennis court and made a garden there including a pond. He would come up to tend it from time to time. His parents, Vernon and Vola, would visit occasionally: Vernon was brother to my grandfather, Grampie. Another brother was Harry, married to Marguerite, and both had been POWs in Japan. They visited with their daughter Kiki, a year younger than us, who was good friends with Robin. Penny Higgs, originally from Jamaica, also came to visit and stay.

THIRTEEN

Macmillan to Douglas-Home: 1955–1963

The heavy defeat for Labour in 1955 caused another call for reappraisals by the party and my father would play a leading role in this process. His majority in Smethwick continued to fall and was now down to 6,500. Despite this, by 1958, there were some suggestions in the press that my father could be the next Labour leader, were Gaitskell to lose the next election – Bevan being too old and Harold Wilson too young. He appealed to newspapers as someone who would not frighten the horses, unlike some Labour MPs. He launched an attack on the Conservatives about a confusion between ministers working for the government and for the party. He attacked the Tories' cynical use of public relations companies, then a novelty. He accused them of using American advertising tactics, anathema then. My father received more favourable press.

It was also mooted that my father might hold high office if Labour returned to power. After all, only he and Wilson had held office before. He was seen as Gaitskell's unofficial chief of staff and was talked of as a future home secretary, foreign secretary or another senior cabinet minister. Gaitskell and my father both lived in or near Hampstead and both believed that Labour must be a party of power, not merely of protest – where have we heard this in recent years? My father called for market research to find where Labour had gone wrong and in an article in *Forward*, he proposed a weakening of the party's links with the TUC and the unions, though the article was watered down. Both Gaitskell and my father believed that Labour was appealing to a working class that no longer existed and that it had to modernise its policies – a foretaste of Tony Blair?

The struggle focused on two issues: Labour's constitution and its defence policy. Gaitskell's personality was not yet known by the general public and my father tended to work in the shadows – he was seen as a real power behind Gaitskell's throne. He was sure of the importance of maintaining control of the party's cumbersome machine, which was not really fit for purpose. He also saw the pitfalls of an opposition committing itself to policies which would be hard to apply when they returned to power.

The real debate centred on Clause Four. The relevant clause was: to secure for the workers by hand or by brain the full fruits of their industry and the most equitable distribution thereof that may be possible upon the basis of the common ownership of the means of production, distribution and exchange, and the best obtainable system of popular administration and control of each industry or service. Earlier my father had suggested that further nationalism should not be a matter of principle, but done only to promote efficiency. 'Social ownership' might mean ownership by local authorities or co-operatives. Should Clause Four be adapted to read 'ownership or control'? Gaitskell was prepared to run with it and a special conference was called in 1959, but the timing was not propitious and support for Clause Four throughout the party – and the unions – was genuine and non-negotiable. Gaitskell said he wanted to add the New Testament to the Old: Harold Wilson instead said that it was rather like trying to take Genesis out of the Bible. The motion was lost and it was to take the skill of Tony Blair to succeed where Gaitskell had failed before.

A fudged set of words was accepted, to save Gaitskell from losing face, but the real battle had been lost. Neither side of the party was satisfied. The left was angered by the attempt and the right was angered by the loss. The Campaign for Democratic Socialism (CDS) was born within the Labour Party and my father was one of its leading lights. It moved from being anti-

Gaitskell to being firmly pro-Gaitskell – it was in some way to lead to the formation of the SDP, which began with the Lincoln by-election of 1973, when Dick Taverne was unseated and stood successfully for re-election. My father was sympathetic to all its leaders and supporters, but he would never have belonged to it; he was too firmly rooted in the Labour Party to move.

The other major issue dividing the party was the defence policy and in particular, whether Labour should support unilateral nuclear disarmament – an issue that has never been fully resolved. The Campaign for Nuclear Disarmament had been formed in 1958 and soon achieved a close alliance with the Labour Party. It was seized on as a way to depose the party's right-wing leadership. Nye Bevan said that the removal of a nuclear deterrent would send the foreign secretary 'naked into the conference chamber' (There is a cartoon of my father with this slogan, with his modesty covered by a fig-leaf). By 1960, trade union support meant that Gaitskell was defeated on the issue, even with a rousing and spirited performance and the vote was closer than thought.

My father was exhilarated by Gaitskell and believed that members were being won over by the tenor of the speech. He started to work in support of Gaitskell, uniting the CDS behind him. My father's backroom skills united trade unionists and party members, hammering out a policy with the NEC and the TUC, so much so that that he was confident of victory at the next debate and conference. Victory on the nuclear issue was won in the 1961 conference and Gaitskell thanked my father for the 'absolutely vital role' he had played. At last, all seemed set for Gaitskell's Labour Party, with the Conservative Party seemingly in terminal decline.

Tragedy, however, was to strike. A rare virus ended Hugh Gaitskell's life on 18 January 1963. This was a tragedy of course for him and his family, but also for the Labour Party, heading finally towards victory – and for my father, who had pinned his colours completely to the Gaitskell mast. My father's tribute

My father in an official photo, dated June 1962, broadcasting on the BBC German language service, as he had done in the war and continued to do so, as he was fluent in German and it brought in some extra income

was made on the radio the following evening:

I have lost my best friend, almost my oldest friend. So overwhelmed am I by this irreplaceable loss that I cannot begin to envisage ... At his death, he was the leading political personality in the country ... Britain has lost a man who would have been one of our greatest prime ministers.

It is hard to refute this judgement. There was even talk that he had been poisoned by the Russians, to allow a more left-wing leader to take over. After the mourning began the process of electing a new leader. Harold Wilson and my father were the only ex-ministers in the party and there was some talk that my father might stand; he certainly had his supporters, but not enough. He had never built up a following in the party, as he normally operated in the background, getting things done with skill and intelligence. In meetings and discussions, he reluctantly decided to stand aside and allow deputy leader George Brown to fight it out with Wilson, with Jim Callaghan putting down a marker for the future.

George Brown, an engaging man whom my father liked, had a problem that he could not hold his drink and he proved to be no match for the wily Wilson. My father supported Brown, but he was not adept at political intrigue and was no match for George Wigg and Dick Crossman in Wilson's corner. My father was genuinely surprised at Wilson's victory, as he was at the offer of the post of shadow foreign secretary – a post coveted by Brown, which he later achieved. This was the ideal position for my father, but his relationship with Wilson did not have a patch of the rapport he had always had with Gaitskell.

Harold Macmillan, the Edwardian prime minister, had triumphed in his first administration from January 1957 to October 1959, but he was finding the 1960s a different decade, with change in the air. His luck seemed to be running out and he seemed out of touch. The launch of *Private Eye* in 1961 found him an easy target for satire. 'Beyond the Fringe', with Peter Cook, Dudley Moore, Alan Bennett and Jonathan Miller, lampooned Macmillan mercilessly. His wife's long-time affair with Bob Boothby left him unsuitable for dealing with sexual scandals. The first embarrassment was the unmasking of John Vassall as a homosexual and Soviet spy in 1962, though the enquiry showed that he had been active since 1954.

The most damning scandal, however, was the Profumo affair, which showed Macmillan in a poor light, with its cast of Christine Keeler, Mandy Rice-Davies, the Soviet naval attaché Yevgeny Ivanov and the osteopath Stephen Ward, who committed suicide. John Profumo, at the War Office, was rumoured to have shared Keeler with Ivanov, thought to be a spy, at Cliveden around the swimming pool. You could not make it up. It had every scandalous detail that the popular press, *Private Eye* and 'Beyond the Fringe' could ask for. Profumo denied any involvement in Parliament and was then shown to have lied. He had to resign as minister of war and retired to do good works at Toynbee Hall in east London with his wife, the actress Valerie Hobson. Macmillan was overwhelmed and unwell with prostate problems, though not as severely as was made out, which allowed him to resign in October 1963.

Macmillan returned to the family firm of Macmillan Publishers in 1964, which I joined twenty-five years later. He had also worked there from 1945 to 1951 when the Conservatives were in opposition. Macmillan had become chancellor of Oxford University in 1960 when he was prime minister. I remember going to a Christ Church gaudy at which an aged Macmillan, near the end of his life, was the guest speaker. He stood up to speak and said nothing for what seemed an age. Eventually he said: "You all thought I had forgotten what I was to say," and then gave a wonderful speech without notes, with the college alumni giving him a standing ovation. He died soon after on 1 December 1986.

Things got better for Labour when Alec Douglas-Home emerged as party leader and prime minister. Another old Etonian, he really was an Edwardian prime minister and seemed even less fit for office than Macmillan. Rab Butler had been expected at last to triumph, but Macmillan and his advisers stitched up the result to produce one of their own. Later on future Conservative leaders would be voted into office, as with Labour, but not always with better results. In the 1960s a prime minister could no longer sit in the House of Lords, so Douglas-Home renounced his hereditary peerage, won a by-election and took office.

He seemed stiff and out of touch with the cunning pipe-smoking Harold Wilson – though Wilson later admitted that the pipe was an act and he preferred cigars but thought them too elite for the Labour Party. He out-scored Douglas-Home, who before renouncing his peerage had been the 14th Earl of Home. Wilson said he supposed that he might be considered the 14th Mr Wilson, and so it went on. Douglas-Home undertook the abolition of retail price maintenance and had small successes in his brief tenure, but he was to prove to have only just under a year in office, serving from 19 October 1963 to 16 October 1964.

When the general election was called on 15 October 1964, Labour assumed that they would achieve a landslide victory. Suez, Vassall, Profumo and the 14th Earl and thirteen years in power had worn out the Conservatives. I recall a Labour Party jamboree at Wembley where Humphrey Lyttelton set a piece of music to which we all sang the refrain 'thirteen wasted years'. The landslide was, however, not to take place and a personal disaster lay ahead for my father, which was to derail everything he had worked for all his political life.

FOURTEEN

Family: 1959–1963

We were all aware of my father's political battles and the periods of opposition. We were older and, when back from school, visited the constituency more, which was changing in nature with increased immigration. My parents used to hold garden parties for political friends – Roy Jenkins, Dick Taverne, Douglas Jay, Bill Rodgers and others on the right of the party. The SDP was almost formed in such gatherings. The family children who were there used to take around eats and drink and the more friendly guests always had a word with us. Douglas Jay used to be fond of the daughters of his political colleagues and he took a shine to Judy. The early introduction to senior politicians meant that I was not in awe of them, and I subsequently published autobiographies by Roy Jenkins and Bill Rodgers.

Judy was married by then and her husband, Graham Greene, was wealthy. On his father's side he was connected to the Greene King brewery and his mother was a Guinness. For once, we received generous Christmas presents and they gave my parents a stair carpet as ours had worn out and there were only bare boards. They lived in Lancaster Gate and then in splendour in Walton Street, Chelsea. Graham was a publisher at Jonathan Cape. Carol had married David Brierley in 1960 and they lived in a flat in the rougher end of Notting Hill, which was certainly potentially violent then, before moving out of London. With some help from my parents, they moved to Kings Langley in Hertfordshire, an old farm with lots of land, to which we were all invited for splendid summer and Boxing Day parties. David was a copywriter in an ad agency and a budding author and fulfilled his ambition later on. He was involved in the launch of the first McDonald's restaurant in England. Cousin Andrew married Juliet Pritchett in April 1966.

Cousin Margaret Susan as a young bridesmaid at a family wedding

Both Judy and Carol were married in the splendid crypt of the House of Commons, where Robin and I had been christened. It was a privilege then reserved for the children of an MP. Robin and I had found attending St Jude's in South Square so tedious and boring that we had become altar boys – acolytes who carried candles either side of the crucifer carrying the cross. We repeated this at Judy's wedding and very splendid we looked!

Ann was ending her time at North London Collegiate and in 1963 was looking to choose a university to continue reading the sciences. She was clever, but maybe not as smart as her elder sisters at Oxford. She failed to find the university of her choice but got into Dundee University through clearing. She still suffered from being the middle child of five, with her elder sisters married and her younger brothers away at school.

Robin and I were at Wellington for this period, from 1959 to 1963 for me and 1964 for Robin. Robin had passed in with much better Common Entrance marks than me and was in higher streams that meant he would do university entrance in the sixth form. I was destined to be a year behind and finish with A-Levels in my last year and head off, as many boys did, to the army or Cirencester Agricultural College. There was one chance of moving up to Robin's grade by the 'remove' system, meaning only five terms for O-Level, not six. I determined to work very hard and managed to make the switch and catch Robin up. Robin, who did not have to work so hard, took his eye off the ball and would not even read the set books, meaning that I achieved better marks than him – the tortoise and the hare. In our first year my grandfather Grampie died. Being deaf, it had been hard to build up a strong relationship with him, but he was a fine man and a balance to Didi, who now ruled supreme at home, always a burden for my mother.

I think Robin was more traumatised by the shock of Wellington than I was. When we arrived, it was not an academic school, with two army sixth forms and one other which was more academic. The new headmaster was determined to start the process of a proper education and we benefited from this. There were now heads of all major subjects and a proper standard of teaching. The army was reducing its size post-war and all those below a certain rank were being pensioned off. They were telling their sons that the new army was not for them, but many disbelieved them and still headed for Sandhurst. The CCF corps and sport were crucial and unavoidable, as was the notion of house spirit, designed to prepare one for the army. I was a natural rebel and was once punished for dumb insolence – the catch-all when prefects wanted to punish you but did not have a specific cause.

Our father and his brother Uncle Robin had been stars of sport and academe and we could not live up to their example. We did our best at sport, having to play rugby, hockey and cricket, and take part in athletics and cross-country running. Robin was taller than me when we started and stronger at sport and was made captain of the house junior cricket team. Things did not work well, so he was replaced by me – another example of how it would have been better if we had been in different houses, as we would seldom have met, only in the classroom and the sports field. I was determined to work to make the most of what was then a boring process of learning by rote and cramming for exams. Robin entered a kind of dream-world and did not seem to get involved; by this stage we were scarcely speaking and suffering from being together both at school and all holidays. Wellington was still a tough school with bullying and endless punishments, but as you worked your way up, you learnt to work the system. It is all so different now, so they say: there are girls and well-being is a core subject.

Our parents only visited us occasionally, as they were busy. We would have a painful Sunday lunch at the Cricketers' Inn, where at every table were boys with their parents – it was only at the end that exeats came in. Judy and Graham sometimes came to take us out. They studied the new *Good Food Guide* and once we went to a pub in Reading, which was a rare treat. Robin complained that it did not have a carpet, unlike the Odeon cinema-type one at the Cricketers'. I left at Christmas 1963, with a place at Christ Church, mainly courtesy of the influence of my father. Robin stayed on, having achieved only one A-Level. If he had got one more A-Level the next year, there was a chance he could go to Oxford, but it was not to be. He instead went as as one of the first students to the University of East Anglia – the only one of us not to go to Oxford, as Ann did a second degree at Oxford, where she met her husband Andy Ball.

At home, Robin and I at last had separate rooms, moving up to the top floor, which had been the domain of our sisters before they left home and married. It made a big difference. In the Suburb, there were many friends of my parents who had children of our age and dances and social events were arranged in school holidays. The Scaddings, the Willises and the Rolls lived in South Square. Eric Roll was a particular friend of my parents, a top economist and civil servant who became the first permanent secretary in Harold Wilson's new Department of Economic Affairs; I used to go out with his daughter, Liz. We bought their Morris 1000 convertible, ER 17, as the first car that my mother had in her own right. There were the Myerings, where Carol's husband- to-be went to lodge, the Rodgerses, with pretty daughters, and Norman and Sarah Collins, already mentioned.

My father had a few long-term friends, mainly from Oxford. Dunstan – who had been his best man – and Elisabeth Skilbeck were friends of both my parents. He was known as Dustpan and my mother was Orge (maybe short for Orgy?). They were always laughing and went away on holidays together. There were the Pages: Denys used to come with my father, Robin and me to Lord's or the Oval, enjoyable occasions – he was an engaging and clever man, who had been a don with my father before becoming master of Jesus College in Cambridge. The Meades were other good friends with whom my father kept in touch. There were also close political friends, but a friend today can stab you in the back or the front tomorrow. Hugh Gaitskell, Roy Jenkins, Dick Rodgers and Shirley Williams remained good friends always, and this raises the possibility that my father would have been sympathetic to the SDP, formed just after his death. But he always told me he would remain loyal to Labour and would talk of one Labour MP, Sir Hartley Shawcross, being nicknamed by others, including my father, Sir Shortly Floor-Cross – which he did do, joining the Conservatives.

My mother kept the show on the road in the house. My father belonged to the generation when men gardened, looked after the car and the bins and worked or studied, while the mother looked after the children, the house, visiting relations and the cooking –

it still continues now. From time to time, relations of Didi's came to stay. There was Doreen, daughter of Didi's sister Rachel, who lived in Canada and whose marriage had ended, and one or two others. Charlotte Chrestien, whose marriage to John Chrestien had also ended, came to stay and they were joined by Joan, who had married my mother's brother Neville and came over to see her family. When he retired, he bought a boat and sailed in it to a new life in Portugal. When Doreen, Charlotte and Joan were staying, my father used to refer to them collectively as the 'abandoned women' and left it for my mother to look after them. Joan was used to heavy drinking in South Africa, and we always said that my father hid the gin when she was on her way. I was fond of all of them and particularly my godfather Neville, who rarely visited, as England had never been his home, and had left after his university studies. My mother and Neville had never been close when growing up in Jamaica.

We began to go on holidays, my parents, Ann and the twins. In 1960 we went to Scotland, with the car on the train to Fort William. We went to Mallaig and Oban, Edinburgh and Kinloch Rannoch, where we unfortunately met our housemaster with a group of boys from Wellington cramming for exams. We would light a fire on the beach before swimming, to warm us up when we came out of the sea. In 1961, we went to Norfolk, where we took a cottage and Graham and Judy joined us for part of the holiday. It was near Walberswick and close enough to the sea to swim. My mother spent the first week cleaning the cottage and the second re-cleaning so no-one would think we had left it unclean – not very restful for all. In 1962, my parents and the youngest children went abroad to the Costa Brava. The car was put on the train to Narbonne, and we drove from there to Tossa del Mar, already built up then, but nothing like it became. We had a sun and swimming holiday, a real treat.

In 1961, Dora (Dodo) Chrestien, my father's mother died, aged seventy-five. My father was the only surviving child, his brother Robin having died so tragically young. I assume there was quite an inheritance for him. We children each received a small legacy, which my parents decided on our behalf to spend on a Swan Hellenic cultural cruise to Greece and Turkey on the SS *Ankara*. Ann and the two boys shared an inside cabin, and my parents had an outside one. It could have been painful, but it was a huge success. My father knew all the guest speakers, who were academics and experts on the places we visited. Mortimer Wheeler was a great lecturer on architecture and the sites we went to: he loved entertaining those on board, especially young and pretty girls. Maurice Bowra was another fascinating lecturer. He was the dean of Wadham College, Oxford, and knew my father well. He was a confirmed bachelor, and a wag accused him of committing the sin of 'Wadomy'. Norman Collins and his wife were also guests on the cruise, and we joined our parents

In 1963, my parents, Ann, Robin and I went on a Swan Hellenic cruise. Here is my father on a small donkey on the island of Patmos

My parents at an exhibition of John Chrestien, an excellent artist and a relation of my paternal grandmother, Dora Chrestien. My parents bought several of his paintings and I have one of these on display at home

with their friends, as well as playing chess as we cruised along. There were enough young people, particularly Americans, to make it fun for us. The thing I remember vividly was that gin and tonic was just tenpence, as there was no tax on board. It was hard to get up some days in time to go on the excursions.

When we reached Athens, my parents were invited to dinner at the British embassy, as my father was shadow foreign secretary. The young were decanted to the ambassador's summer residence near Piraeus with his children and we had an enjoyable evening with them. It was a holiday that everyone enjoyed immensely.

FIFTEEN

Smethwick: 1963–1964

In 1963, Alec Douglas-Home was clearly not going to last long, and my father had been shadow foreign secretary for some time under Harold Wilson. He realised that after Suez, Great Britain's influence was on the wane. Alliances were essential, in Europe, of which he was a passionate supporter, the USA and the Commonwealth, after the effects of Macmillan's 'winds of change'. My father was being courted as a de facto foreign secretary and it was clear to us that this was the job for which he was ideally suited. All sorts of people sought influence and he was perhaps rather naïve about the motives of some. I remember an Italian who invited my parents to Rome and my mother said she could not go as I was at home – a lame excuse as I was nearly an adult and my grandmother was at home. So, I was invited too, all expenses paid, and put up at the Hassler Hotel by the Spanish Steps.

There were no formal gap years at that time, but there were nine months between school and university. In January 1964, I was sent to the University of Grenoble for a term to learn French. I did not have enough money, as usual, and lived in a cheap hall of residence with only French students, which was later used to house skiers for the 1968 winter Olympics. I learnt some French, though people thought I was from Marseilles, as my French was similar to the English spoken by a Geordie. I got some skiing but 1964 was one of the years when there was little snow.

In the summer of 1964, Robin and I went with my parents to Naples as guests of Charles Forte and his family, whose luxury yacht was moored in the bay. A more worldly politician would have realised that there was a risk in accepting such generosity from a businessman and hotelier. Robin and I put such thoughts

I am off with my parents on a trip to Rome, as they said they could not leave their son behind! Note my 'smart' raincoat. My parents were busy with political meetings, so I was free to enjoy the city

to one side and enjoyed a splendid holiday at a smart hotel and we were often invited on the Forte yacht, with Rocco and his beautiful sisters. There were tender craft and water skis for all to enjoy. Rocco went up to Oxford in my year and I met him again when he had got his Cadillac stuck in a narrow lane and a team of us had to bounce it out, with considerable damage. He was a champion fencer and went on to run the family hotel business. The Naples trip was splendid in every way, far better than the built-up holiday on the Costa Brava, with its busy beaches.

My father was busy in meetings and trips to Europe, to see world leaders. I was back from France and living at home during this period. There was a real sense that the political tide was moving to Labour. There was the rally at Wembley with its refrain of 'thirteen wasted years'. The same mood applied to Labour as it did in 1994, when Margaret Thatcher had been succeeded by John Major and Labour was ready under Tony Blair. The Conservatives had a similar anticipation after Gordon Brown, even though it only led to a coalition.

However exciting the feeling was for Labour, on a personal level the omens were not good for Smethwick. My father could not spend as much time in the constituency as perhaps he should, as he was shadowing the Foreign Office. At each of the elections under the Conservatives, his majority had fallen. In 1951 it was a safe 9,727, then in 1955 it fell to 6,495 and in 1959 it was just 3,544. There was also the issue of race, which was ripe to be exploited for the first time. Much was to be made of the fact that my mother had been born in Jamaica, which did not help support for the Labour Party. Race was to become a major political issue in future politics as it was with the Brexit referendum. But only with hindsight could one have predicted what was to happen, though my father was aware that the constituency was changing.

In early October 1964, I began my university career at Christ Church and was there for the general election. I had watched every election at home since they were televised and stayed up all night for every one. The college's only television was in the Junior Common Room. A group of mainly Conservative supporters – this was Christ Church, after all – including Alec Douglas-Home's son David, Quintin Hogg's son Douglas and Gerald Nabarro's son Rupert, were all watching as the results came in. The consensus was that Labour would win by a landslide but it became clear that this was not to be – the Tory natural majority in rural areas and southern towns was holding up better than expected.

It was just before midnight, when many had called it a day, that the result from Smethwick came in, with my father losing by 1,774 votes to Peter Griffiths, the Conservative candidate. It was sensational and I felt physically sick: I cannot envisage the bombshell effect this must have had on my parents, at the count in the Town Hall. Everything my father had worked for since

Oxford politics went in the blink of an eye. Even nearly sixty years on, I still remember the trauma that effectively ended my father's political career.

I finally went to bed with a heavy heart. In those days there were of course no mobile phones, and I could not contact my parents or siblings that evening or the next morning. The salt in the wound was that most people in Christ Church were pleased and believed that maybe the Conservatives would hold on; the final Labour majority was only five, but a majority it was after thirteen years of Conservative rule. The next day, the result in Smethwick was front page news and in all the broadcasts and a Labour post-mortem began. I discovered only later that my father had warned Gaitskell in 1962 that Smethwick might be in danger. I had not been to the constituency for quite some time and so was not aware of the changing dynamic.

Smethwick had in the 1950s seen an influx of British citizens from the West Indies and India. It was not alone in the new phenomenon, but Smethwick had industries to attract workers and coloured immigration had become a political issue. At the start of the 1960s, the Birmingham Immigration Control Association was founded and in 1961, a Smethwick branch was formed. My father claimed that better housing and facilities would help the issue, but he was particularly vulnerable, because as Labour's Commonwealth spokesman, he had opposed the government's Commonwealth Immigration Bill of 1961. He was right to oppose it, but the far right exploited the situation; slogans appeared on a Sikh temple – 'N****rs out', 'Gordon Walker traitor' and 'Long Live England'. I knew about some of this at the time, as did my older sisters, who spent time in the constituency helping my father in his campaign.

The Tories did well in the local elections of 1962 and better in 1963. I remember hearing that my father accused the Tories of arranging for children to parade around the streets shouting: 'If you want a n****r neighbour, vote Labour.' My father was a social democrat and instinctively favoured immigration with less controls than the Conservatives wanted and there is no doubt that the Tories exploited the situation for political gain. Rumours were spread that my father had sold his constituency home to immigrants – he did not have one to sell – that his wife was black, coming from Jamaica, and that his daughters had married black men. He was accused, along with Gaitskell, who was dead by now, of being pro-immigration.

A punchier candidate than my father might have fought back harder – it was fate and the death of the sitting MP in 1945 that had brought him to Smethwick. The Conservative candidate in 1959, when race was not such an issue, was Peter Griffiths; in 1964, with Griffiths still the Tory candidate, things were very different. My father fought back on race and at an open-air meeting he suggested that immigration to Smethwick was indeed too high and should be spread more evenly over the Midlands. But Smethwick had industrial jobs and that is why immigrants settled there. Perhaps my father might have been better to stress the efforts the local council was taking to provide financial aid to areas of high immigration and better housing, but he could not, by temperament or oratorical skill, match Griffiths's populism. Other Tory MPs from the Midlands, including Edward Boyle and even Enoch Powell, refused to help Peter Griffiths, though Powell was later to harden his views.

In the election, there was nationally a swing to Labour of 3.5 per cent, but in Smethwick, a rare Tory win, the swing to the Conservatives was 7.2 per cent. Griffiths claimed that my father had lost because the Hampstead Garden Suburb academic candidate was out of touch with local needs and problems. There may be an element of truth in this, but he was an assiduous visitor to Smethwick and aware through councillors and his constituency of what the concerns were, but he may not have been the best candidate to counter the race allegations, which were to bedevil both parties hereafter. Harold Wilson dubbed Griffiths the 'parliamentary leper' but I do not think that he would have been much concerned by this accusation.

SIXTEEN

Foreign Secretary to Leyton: 1964–1965

The family rallied to my father's side as soon as they could, and he had political advisers like John Harris to help. Wilson had promised to make my father foreign secretary and he honoured this promise, even though my father did not have a seat. A new one had to be found for him, where an aged MP could be persuaded to stand down, and this had to be a quick process.

In the meantime, he moved into the Foreign Office and met the team there. He attended a crisis meeting of the European Free Trade Association (EFTA) and in December 1964 went for talks at the White House. Perhaps the most important issue was a change in Labour's defence policy, the acceptance of Polaris submarines.

The foreign secretary's residence is, and was, No. 1 Carlton Gardens, a fine building at the far end of the Gardens from Trafalgar Square, in a cul de sac for safety. I came down from Oxford to see the residence, which was on two floors above lavish entertainment floors – certainly grander than South Square in Hampstead Garden Suburb. My elder sisters were married, and Ann was at Dundee, but I remember Ann, Robin and I being there for Christmas 1964. Robin had stayed on at school for final exams and I was down from my first term at Oxford. The downstairs floor of the flat had reception and dining rooms and the floor above had the bedrooms – I was no longer sharing with Robin. It seemed very opulent to us and quite restrictive as there were police downstairs and a concierge checking on who was coming and going. There was not time for many friends to visit, though a way was worked out whereby girls could be smuggled in – the major threat was from my mother, not from the guards.

At New Year, we visited the foreign secretary's country residence, which in those days was Dorneywood, a National Trust property in Buckinghamshire. The couple who ran it made it clear that Rab Butler was much more to their liking than the Labour Patrick Gordon Walker, though my father was every bit as grand as Rab. It was not relaxing there. Each meal had to be negotiated and everything had to be paid for. It had lavish grounds, and a squash court in the stable block, where my father beat me, even though I had played regularly at Wellington and was to do so at Christ Church. It turned out that there was only to be the one visit.

The by-election, at Leyton, was set for 21 January 1965. We all went down to visit and to help, as it was conveniently close. Reg Sorensen, the sitting MP, was seventy-three and did not want to stand down; he did not believe in peerages, so there was nothing to offer him in return. The omens seemed a bit worrying, because the National Front had taken up the mantle of using the race card, but with a vengeance. Colin Jordan, leader of the National Socialist Movement, was responsible for slogans which were daubed on walls: 'Walker Gordon. The race mixing candidate. Make Britain black.' At the first public meeting there were calls of 'Go back to Jamaica'. Jordan dressed as a monkey with the slogan 'We immigrants are voting for Gordon Walker' and giving a Nazi salute.

Again, my father was the wrong man at the wrong time. He gave off a lofty disdain which was not a true reflection, but he was not good at public speaking and at talking to the man in the street. He looked sad and could not change his expression and solemn photos appeared in the press. Perhaps he should have become Pat Walker. He was faced with continued playing of the race card as he had been at Smethwick and experienced far worse personal attacks than did most candidates. There was also some resentment that the local candidate, who was certainly more at ease with the people of Leyton, had been pushed aside, to make room for the foreign secretary. It was a miscalculation to choose this seat, and

The family gathered at a constituency dinner dance in Leyton, Christmas 1964. At one table are my parents, with the constituency agent to the right of my mother [top left]. *At another table, Robin facing the camera and Carol, with glasses, on the right* [top right]. *At another table is Judy, left in white, then Ann's boyfriend at the time, with glasses and then Ann* [bottom left]. *Finally, me and next to me with a shawl is Didi, my mother's mother who lived with us* [bottom right].

his Foreign Office advisers proved not to be up to the job.

We were in the Town Hall for the result, and to the amazement and deep shock of all of us and Labour supporters, my father was defeated by 205 votes. His career was in ruins. He had had a chance after the Smethwick defeat, but there was no way back now. He had to resign at once, having been foreign secretary for only a few months, the job for which he was best suited. There was some talk of standing in Abertillery, with a 20,000 Labour majority and certainly no race issues, except possibly for Welsh ones. But he had had enough. He was an unlucky politician. He was praised for his dignity in the face of a crushing defeat and heart-breaking disappointment. The last word at Leyton for this election was from an elderly woman who said she would not be voting for 'that Lucky Gordon Walker' – confusing him with Lucky Gordon – 'that was in the Christine Keeler case'!

SEVENTEEN

Interregnum: 1965–1966

My parents, Ann, Robin and I had to vacate Carlton Gardens to accommodate the new foreign secretary, Michael Stewart. Our house, 22 South Square, had been on the market during this period, but with no takers, which was fortuitous – the property market was not as it is now. We were not sorry to be shot of Dorneywood. With our tails between our legs, we headed home to lick our wounds. My father never showed any emotion to us and did not talk about the tragedy that had hit him, though he may have done so in private. It would have been better for all if he had. For my mother, tragedy had hit her twice and what happened was out of her control, which is harder to take. Looking back, I believe that she had a nervous breakdown, though there were no obvious symptoms we could detect – she was always nervy and worried. When we were young the doctor did not tell her what was wrong with us. For example, my whooping cough as a child was put down to growing pains and my infantile asthma was to return later in life.

Our doctor, Joe Stone, was a sole practitioner, who still made home visits; he was also Harold Wilson's doctor. When Wilson became prime minister, Dr Stone became his official doctor. It was suggested that when Wilson was having difficulty with his aide Marcia Falkender, Stone offered, I hope jokingly (according to Bernard Donoughue, a political aide to Wilson, in his book), that he could find a way to remove her 'permanently' – fortunately it never happened

My mother had supported my father all the way, been on many trips with him, and now it was gone. We did what we could, but the elder two sisters were married and the rest of us were away at university. We did come back for vacations and tried to help. My grandmother Didi was still there, which was now more of a burden than a help. She had rheumatoid arthritis and was increasingly lame, but she could be as annoying as ever. Whenever tensions with my mother grew beyond repair, she would take herself off to Barnes, where Sheila Bower, her niece lived in a flat, and stay with her. It was a long journey from the Suburb, and I used to visit her and try to cheer her up. When Sheila had had enough, Didi came back home. It cannot have been easy for Didi being dependent on us all, but she made sure that we were all there to help.

My father had, as foreign secretary, agreed to undertake a fact-finding mission for the government in Southeast Asia – going to Laos and Hanoi, to the USA to continue talks about Vietnam, and to other countries where American influence was strong – and to report back to Wilson and the Foreign Office. This trip gave him something worthwhile to get his teeth into and he was well suited for this. He was committed to fight Leyton again at the next general election, which could not be far off, as it was almost impossible to continue for long with a majority of five. He had to visit the constituency and try to build up support ready for when he stood again. During this period, my father had time on his hands for the first time for decades. He still wrote articles and did broadcasts for German TV on British issues – he remained fluent in German and not bad in French. He was assisted by his good friend Werner Rolfe, who worked for German TV based in London and offered him lucrative assignments like covering general elections.

My parents joined the Suburb Institute, a few minutes away, which provided adult education. They both learnt painting and we all were given examples of their work – I still have mine as does my sister Carol in her nursing home. My mother's painting was true to life and more like a photograph, while my father's style was more impressionistic. There were walks on the Heath, tennis and croquet, holidays to Crete and Turkey, and my father kept up with political friends during this period.

A happy picture of my father in 1965, when he took on some overseas trips in the interregnum. Here he is on the MV Leda *in Bergen, September 1965*

During vacations, Ann, Robin and I returned home and spent time with my father, Robin and I often playing chess with him. Looking back, my mother was a pale imitation of herself and was never to recover her poise in full. It was as if the trauma of coming over from Jamaica to Oxford had returned to haunt her. My father was essentially depressed too, though, like many men, he supressed his feelings and channelled them into outward pursuits, like sport, and inward ones, like reading and chess.

My father was offered the position of head of the Book Development Council (BDC), a quango designed to encourage publishers, booksellers and overseas trade, which did worthwhile work promoting the book trade. This came about through a combination of his old friend and neighbour in the Suburb, Eric Roll, and Judy's husband, Graham Greene, managing director of Jonathan Cape publishers. The BDC no longer exists as a separate entity.

I was away at Oxford, where I had many friends and played rugby and cricket. It was a time of rebellion and sport was not as popular as it had been especially at a college level, though we put out reasonable teams. I made masses of friends: also a time when one had more time than money. When I went up in October 1964, my father's income was augmented by being a cabinet minister. In my second term and onward, I was on a maximum grant from my local council (there were no up-front fees in those days), with help from my parents with living costs, but I was poor by Christ Church standards. There were many there with enormous incomes, who could belong to every club and society. However, I never felt deprived and made very good friends – it was all men at the college in those days – quite a few of whom I have kept for life.

Many of these friends came to South Square and met my parents, sometimes playing tennis with my father. Men in Oxford hugely out-numbered girls, so there were sixth-form and secretarial colleges to try to help make up for the shortfall.

My father was a great gardener and here he is in front of his rose bed, around 1965. His cravat matched the roses

It was said that it was easy to find someone to go out with from Monday to Thursday, but much harder at the weekend. In those days it was possible to go to prep school, public school and Oxbridge, then the Bar and men's clubs – and scarcely meet a girl until the time came to marry, often a sister of a male friend. It can still happen now.

I only saw Robin in vacations, as Norwich, where he was at the University of East Anglia, to Oxford was quite a journey. I never went to Dundee to see Ann. All of us met for Christmas and were invited to a wonderful regular Boxing Day lunch by David and Carol at Kings Langley. The family diverged, but we were always there for anyone who needed help. I do not now recall how much I saw my parents during 1965, though I must have been with them in the long summer vacation. We were all aware that the disaster that had befallen my father meant that it would be very hard for him to rebuild a long-term political future. The Foreign Office had been the perfect job for him, a big position but not a spending department, in which he would have had little experience. (The Conservatives, with their experience of big business, normally fared better with such departments.) There was no guarantee, anyway, that he would get back into office. Labour had performed poorly in council elections in 1965 and lost a by-election, so their working majority was down to two. In the same year, Alec Douglas-Home stood down and was replaced by Edward Heath, who had little charisma but was a serious party leader, but he had only eight months to make his mark.

EIGHTEEN

Leyton and Victory: March 1966

The Conservatives claimed that they were unprepared for a snap election after eighteen months, but it was clear that Labour needed a real mandate, even if it risked them going out of office. Parliament was dissolved on 28 February 1966, leaving a month for campaigning. My father had had ample time to prepare and had been out of the public eye for this period. The public had not seen his melancholy dignity and bloodhound disposition for some time.

The date for the election of 1966 was fixed for 31 March. This coincided with the Easter vacation for Robin and me and so we spent nearly every day in late March canvassing and organising canvassing. Ann came down too, and Judy and Carol. Robin was there most of the time, but I based myself in Leyton. My Oxford friend John Heskett came to help. His mother's car, which she had lent him, was plastered with Labour stickers and those specific to my father and we drove it round the constituency. He lived at his parents' house in Reigate, where they weigh the Conservative votes rather than count them. Once when he was parking the car on the front drive a policeman came by and said: 'If I were you, sir, I would park your car in the garage.'

We had no way of knowing what the outcome would be, but the race issue seemed to have died down. With a general election, protest groups had to spread themselves country-wide, whereas in a by-election, protest can be focused much more exactly. There had been such an outcry about Smethwick, and then Leyton in 1965, that racism was somewhat kept in check. There was a feeling of quiet optimism, but twice before, we had assumed victory for my father. I have a JAK cartoon of him standing on a hustings, looking aloof and unhappy as a Conservative candidate leans out of a Mini and shouts through a megaphone: 'Third time lucky, Patrick?' We hoped so.

Robin and I added another football team to the ones we supported, Crystal Palace and West Bromwich Albion: the pleasingly named Leyton Orient. A couple of times, when we had despatched the volunteer canvassers, we sloped off to the terraces to watch the team, getting back to the party offices in time for the canvassers' return, but we all worked pretty hard. Even though it was just one constituency, it attracted press and broadcasters from the UK and abroad, sensing the possibility of another upset. I helped to co-ordinate the media interest, selecting those I thought would be right for my father to respond to, an interesting and helpful process.

The day of polling finally arrived. We canvassed until the day before and the omens seemed good this time. There was quiet expectation that there would be a victory for the Labour Party and in Leyton, which had hitherto been a safe Labour seat, but the size of any majority would not be clear until the count. I remember that we were quietly confident, but we did not count our chickens. Counting took place all evening and Robin and I were monitors. We soon saw that the Labour votes were stronger than for other candidates, including those for the Conservative candidate, Ronald Buxton, who had won the by-election of 1965.

The result was a return to normal for Leyton. My father was returned with a majority of 8,646. Both my parents were ecstatic, and the press and TV finally showed some photos of my father smiling, which had not been done in 1964 or 1965. The country felt that Labour had not had a real chance with virtually no majority and a difficulty in governing. Labour achieved a majority of ninety-eight seats, pretty much a landslide, and the party's vote rose by 3.9 per cent. It was on a par with 1945 and Harold Wilson was secure for now. Smethwick also returned to the Labour fold, with the actor Andrew Faulds defeating the 'parliamentary leper', Peter Griffiths; he was returned to Parliament for Portsmouth North from 1979 to 1997, but his notoriety was over.

Wilson promised my father a return to the cabinet, but what job would he be offered? Would Wilson recognise his abilities? He had been in the cabinet back in 1950 and had great experience, but there was no way in which he was returning to the Foreign Office. A reshuffle was due, but it would not take place for quite a time, until January 1967, nine months later.

A cartoon by Jak, 1966, ironically wishing my father good luck in the general election at Leyton

NINETEEN

Return to Cabinet: 1967

My father was back in the House of Commons, with an MP's salary, but sitting on the back benches. He had to bide his time. He still earned money by reviewing, writing and broadcasting, as being a backbench MP is not a full-time job, as is abundantly clear today, but he was never involved in lobbying. The total remuneration for an MP when my father was in the House was not a patch on the package available later.

Having achieved our goal, Robin and I returned to our respective universities. I was halfway through my second year, still living in college and having a good time. In the long vacations, we went on holidays, mainly in Europe, to Tuscany my first year, Corsica the next, and one Easter holiday, Robin and I drove in my mother's car back to Naples where we had been on a holiday earlier with our parents. We were not on the best of terms always, having seen quite enough of each other all our life, but later went back to being good friends.

The drawback of living in the Suburb was that we were cut off from London, with a long walk to the Tube and a long walk back – and the Tube and buses closed in the evenings much earlier then. On one occasion, I was invited with several friends to an amazing party given by a popular girl at Oxford, whose father was a diamond tycoon. I drove into London to the celebrated Speakeasy nightclub where it was held. Both the Hollies and the Move pop groups had been booked; drinks of whatever variety were free. I woke up the next morning in South Square, with four other friends and no recollection of how I had got back – there were no breathalysers then, but it was still foolish.

I often saw my father and he was not overtly bitter about the way his career had panned out. He was still in denial and did not really want to talk about it and buried himself in work. He used to reread an author as he went to sleep, such as Trollope or Dickens. Bit by bit, in a year he would have read all the books of the chosen author. With a photographic memory, he could recall all that he read. He watched sport on television, reserved for the BBC in those days. My parents rather rattled around in the big house, but we returned regularly to see them. We played croquet and there were always good meals on tap. A young Austrian girl called Maria had come to us to help, having been rescued from a home nearby where she was being exploited. She stayed on for many years, being offered a secure home. When we were grown up, she became a companion and looked after my grandmother, Didi, still living with us. My father was rather marking time, waiting hopefully for the promised reshuffle.

Eventually my father was brought back into the cabinet in January 1967 as minister without portfolio, a far cry from the Foreign Office, but he was glad to be back. His main tasks involved negotiating the British military presence in Malta and taking over the long-term review of social services. He and the then chancellor, Jim Callaghan, eventually agreed to propose a means test for increased family allowances. This would never be popular with elements of the Labour Party, who believed that universal benefits should not be means tested. A compromise was worked out whereby family allowances would rise, but by less for fourth and subsequent children – families were much larger then; I was one of five. Part of the costs came from higher school meal and welfare milk charges and an adjustment for income tax allowances for children. My father had wanted to grasp the nettle of the means test, opposing it, but the government finances were under considerable pressure at this time.

Harold Wilson wanted to offer my father his old job at the CRO (by now the Commonwealth Office), which would have suited him ideally. George Brown, now foreign secretary, however, objected as the two departments worked closely together and in 1968 became one. Brown did not want my father to plead the Commonwealth case and so slow down Britain's entry into the EEC. Brown and my father had been good friends and he had proposed Brown in the leadership battle with Gaitskell. I remember meeting George Brown on several occasions. He was often the worse for wear. It was not that he always drank too much, but more that his metabolism meant it affected him more than others – or that was the party line.

In May 1967, Robin and I celebrated our twenty-first birthday, with a celebration at home and then a reunion of old friends on the terrace of the House of Commons, with the Jay twins, the Page twins and others. It was an interlude for my father in all his political responsibilities.

My parents and Douglas Jay at the celebration of our twenty-first party on the terrace of the House of Commons. There are three sets of twins: Robin and me, Helen and Catherine Jay, either side of my father and Juliet and Rosamond Page, either side of my mother. Their father, Denys Page, was a colleague of my father as a don at Christ Church before becoming Master of Jesus College, Cambridge

Robin's and my 21st birthday, 15 May 1967

Instead of returning to the Commonwealth Office, my father was instead appointed the minister for education in August 1967. This was a big spending department, and, like all ministries at this time, was under pressure to make savings. Any education cuts affected all those with children and hence would be as unpopular as savings in welfare and rises in income tax. I remember having lunch with my father and visiting him at the Education offices; very grand. He got to grip with plans to increase teacher training facilities, following the Plowden report, and expand primary school provision. However, he was unlucky in his timing once again. Following the devaluation of sterling in November 1967 (the pound in your pocket, said Wilson, is still worth the same), the cabinet was forced to agree to a package of cuts. My father had reluctantly to accept the end of free milk in secondary schools ('Margaret Thatcher, milk snatcher', would later end free milk for all schoolchildren) but more was needed. There was a wrangle when the intention to turn the 400-year-old

Enfield Grammar School into a comprehensive was blocked by an injunction. My father was blamed for this debacle.

The cabinet meeting of 5 January 1968 involved a fearful row. In order to save higher education funding, with the backing of Wilson, Dick Crossman, Barbara Castle, Dick Marsh and Peter Shore, my father had to agree to Roy Jenkins's proposal to postpone raising the school leaving age from fifteen to sixteen. Cabinet agreed this by only eleven votes to ten. George Brown, my father's erstwhile friend, led the protests to this cut, exploding: 'May God forgive you. You send your children to university, and you would put the interests of the school kids below that of the universities.' Brown was supported by Callaghan and the university-educated Anthony Crosland and Michael Stewart. The cabinet was divided and the fall-out for my father was not helped by his neighbour in the Suburb, Lord Longford (previously Frank Pakenham), godfather of Judy and an old friend and colleague from Christ Church, resigning as leader of the Lords in protest – a cowardly manoeuvre to escape the battlefield. He went on to produce *The Longford Report* on pornography in 1972, which was a big flop, and Frank never recovered his credibility. He supported Mary Whitehouse and visited famous or infamous people in prison, including Myra Hindley.

To oversee such cuts was not what my father had gone into politics for, but he was in the hot seat and had to agree to major savings as the lesser of the evils on offer. The press turned on him again, and sadly he was not suited to running a big spending department. Personally, I believe that his morale never recovered from the two defeats at Smethwick and Leyton in quick succession. My mother once again faced a crisis, which was to knock her back worse than before. Wilson replaced my father in June 1968 and his political career and position in a cabinet were over for good. He was now sixty years old – people retired earlier in those days. He became a backbencher again and Wilson arranged for him to become a companion of honour – a special accolade. I still have the citation and his crest.

TWENTY

Home Life: 1966–1968

During 1966 and 1967, I was still at Christ Church and Robin at East Anglia. Ann joined me at Oxford for a year, doing a post-doc, and we used to meet up. Both of us were working for final exams, Ann harder than me. My father had to have a delayed hip replacement – too much serious sport when a young man. He took a long time to recover, and my mother was faced with two people hobbling around, my father and Didi. In June 1967, I came down from Oxford and spent time at home. My friend Justin Cartwright knew the manager of a travel company, American Grand Circle, which took American holidaymakers on escorted three-week coach tours throughout Europe. For many of them, this was their first trip out of the USA, and they sought safety in numbers. It was very lucrative for the couriers recruited to accompany the travellers, mainly friends from Oxford. We were paid a small subsistence sum, but the real money came from tips and commission from shops where they bought items, selected by the courier. I kept doing it for six months rather than get a job and made enough to buy a Mini.

Initially, I stayed at my friend Serge Beddington-Behrens's Belgravia flat, as he was staying up an extra year in Oxford to finish his degree. It was incredibly convenient and I stayed there for 1968. It was quite a wild flat, especially for Justin Cartwright's stag night before marrying Penny, and whenever Serge descended from Oxford and reclaimed his room – he was quite a playboy then. Once, driving up the fashionable King's Road in a plastic bubble car, he saw a pretty girl, turned to look at her and crashed into the car in front, and his car collapsed in a heap. He had rented a *finca* in Ibiza at the time and we set off there in my Mini instead. He knew my father and referred to him affectionately as 'Doggie Chops', which was not a bad description, picked up later at his parliamentary defeats.

My parents outside the church after a wedding in the late sixties

Me in front of 22 South Square with my new car, a trendy Triumph Herald convertible. Note the smart attire. Around my 22nd birthday

Jobs were plentiful for graduates in those days, as were unfurnished flats where you had security of tenure. With help from a friend of my father, who was trying to curry favour with him – my father not noticing this, as usual – I was able to rent a two-bedroom flat in a mansion block between Tottenham Court Road and Gower Street and offered a room to my Oxford friend Mike McIntyre, which helped pay for the ridiculously small rent; we stayed there for five years. Mike would sometimes come with me to see my parents, and I knew his. In those times, once you left university, you basically left home or got married, as had Judy and Carol. Ann met her husband-to-be at Oxford, Andrew Ball, and they got married in 1968 and headed to the University in Connecticut, because scientific grants and career possibilities were much greater in the USA than in the UK. Tottenham Court Road to Hampstead Garden Suburb was no distance and I had my car, with no parking restrictions in those days, so I went home a couple of times a week, to see my parents, play chess and watch sport. My father was only sixty-one, but looked older, my mother was fifty-eight.

TWENTY-ONE

Backbenches Again: 1968–1974

My father's relationship with Harold Wilson had been one of convenience and they were not natural political allies. The Wilsons had lived one street from the Gordon Walkers in the Suburb, but I do not recall us meeting, even though both families had children of about the same age, whom we occasionally met, as well as Harold and Mary. Hugh Gaitskell had been my father's natural ally, and some things might well have gone better for my father if Gaitskell had not died so young. As Wilson became increasingly unpopular, faced with difficult issues, my father became a prime mover in the 'Wilson must go' campaign – he had nothing to lose now. Working closely with Ivor Richard, Roy Hattersley, Dick Taverne and Chris Mayhew, my father organised a group of a hundred backbenchers, who would at the right moment seek to replace Wilson with Jim Callaghan, or preferably Roy Jenkins. The right moment, however, never came and Wilson was a wily bird. After Labour's surprising defeat to Edward Heath in 1970, my father switched to supporting Wilson as a bulwark against the anti-EU feeling sweeping the Labour Party. My father was a fervent European and fortunately for him never witnessed Brexit.

My father wrote future obituaries, some of which were used, articles and book reviews both historical and political. He decided not to write an autobiography, perhaps wisely, but instead started work on a book, *The Cabinet*, published in 1970 by Jonathan Cape, the firm run by Graham Greene, married to my sister Judy. It was a serious historical and political study, but engagingly lively and direct. It was enlivened by references to my father's own experiences, but the book was subject to the thirty-year rule, which made events described allusive rather than explicit. It received blanket newspaper coverage and reviews, and the *Daily Mail* pieced together a story, from a footnote about Wilson and Brown being overruled on a matter of great importance, which was assumed to refer to the Arab–Israeli War of 1967, running with the headline 'The Day Wilson Almost Went to War'. My father had to deny this interpretation that his book implied any such reference to that war. The second edition made matters a little clearer. The publicity ensured strong sales, the most of any of the books that he wrote, in hardback and then in paperback from Fontana, then an imprint of William Collins.

Heath survived from 1970 to 1974, with my parents still electioneering for the local party in Hampstead Garden Suburb. In 1973 Heath finally took Britain into the European Communities (EC), of which my father would have approved as a first step towards European unity, but he also presided over the disastrous three-day week when he took on the unions about 'who governed Britain' and lost. There were blackouts and factories and shops were forced to close when the lights went out. The question 'Who governs Britain?' was answered 'Not you'. He was never a popular figure, a bachelor very keen on sailing and music, on which he wrote books. Neither Wilson nor Heath had the charisma of later prime ministers. There were two inconclusive elections in 1974, in February and October. In the first election, Labour gained fourteen seats, but was short of an outright majority, and there was a hung parliament for the first time since 1929. Heath tried and failed to coalesce with the Liberals under Jeremy Thorpe and the Ulster Unionists, and Wilson returned to power, but such a situation could not survive for long. In the first 1974 election, my father stood down as an MP and was elevated to the peerage as Lord Gordon-Walker of Leyton. For the first time for sixty-seven years, he had a hyphen his name in order to keep both his surnames in full. In the October election of the same year, Wilson got an outright majority, and Labour assumed power again.

TWENTY-TWO

Family: 1968–1975

Around 1972, my father still had not fully recovered from his hip operation, and hobbled around and walked with a stick, which I still have. Only three years before, he had regularly being playing tennis. He was also increasingly deaf and wore those headphones that go over your whole ear as he watched the TV – we joked that this was so he could not hear our mother. My grandmother, Didi, also hobbled around with her rheumatism and this all proved too much for my mother, who arranged for Didi to move into a nursing home in Finchley. This broke her heart and visits by family did not help. She assumed that she had been put out to die and die she did in October 1973. She

My father ready for tennis in the doorway of 22 South Square in 1968, aged 61. He was a keen sportsman and played tennis well into his sixties

had been part of the family all my life and longer for Judy and Carol, in exile in Jamaica. She looked after the three younger children when our parents were away travelling or out on official occasions. She could be a difficult person in some ways and was a trial to my mother – my father let it all wash over him.

My father with Stephanie Page at her wedding reception in 1969, at Jesus College, Cambridge. Her father, Denys Page, was an old friend of my parents and was then Master of Jesus College. My mother was Stephanie's godmother

I was very fond of her, having been one of her favourites, and missed her when she was gone.

Ann had got married in 1968, again in the crypt of the House of Commons, to Andrew Ball. Carol had a daughter, Margaret, born in 1970, named after my Uncle Robin's daughter Margaret, who was tragically killed in a car accident on her twenty-first birthday. Carol and David were estranged after Margaret's birth, and Carol and Margaret came to stay with us and the baby and Didi became firm friends. There were plans for Carol and me to buy a house in Highbury and to divide it into two dwellings, but this came to naught. Eventually Carol and little Margaret were reunited with David. Robin married June Barr at a registry office in 1974 and I was his best man. He had joined Thomson Newspapers as a trainee on the *South Wales Echo*, to learn the craft of journalism, which had none of the technology of today, and he was to stay a journalist for most of his career. I was able to live for some time on the proceeds of my American courier job, based at Serge's flat, and there were enough friends about not working full time to play tennis and socialise with. Gradually many friends started jobs, except for the very rich Christ Church and Oxford ones, who did not need to. I remember Justin Cartwright, who wanted to get into advertising, printing some cards saying: 'Justin Cartwright, Director, New Operations' with no company name. It worked.

I wanted to go into publishing. I asked my father for help with my career and he told me that a fellow MP was an accountant, advice I did not follow. My sister Judy had worked in publicity for André Deutsch, her husband Graham Greene was at Jonathan Cape and my father had had several books published. I tried to get in, but it was difficult and I only got negative responses. I asked Graham for advice and he said that publishing was a business and declined to help. I worked in the City for a year, marking time. My flatmate, Michael McIntyre, had found a job at Anthony Blond on the educational side – there were then many eponymous firms there such as Jonathan Cape, Michael Joseph, André Deutsch, Hamish Hamilton, Weidenfeld & Nicolson,

George Duckworth and so on. Michael used to come back stoned early on a Friday afternoon and I determined to try once again. Having a famous name then had its uses and when I wrote again to publishers, I got positive responses, suggesting we met for a chat. The boss of Duckworth had known my Uncle Robin and we had a pub lunch, I also saw the head of Chatto & Windus, but Graham was still not helpful.

Eventually I was asked for interviews by Hodder & Stoughton on the educational editorial side and by Macmillan as a salesman. John Attenborough, the deputy chairman at Hodder, had been on the Book Development Council with my father and got me an interview with the charming head of the educational division and I was offered an editorial traineeship at half the salary I was earning in the City. But I had my foot on the bottom rung and I was in, never to look back. Robin was in Cardiff, Ann was married and soon off to the States and I was in my flat in central London and working near St Paul's. In 1971, I met Louise Harington and there was an instant attraction, at least on my part. It must have been mutual because we have been together ever since.

Until early 1974, my father was still MP for Leyton and we occasionally went to the constituency for social occasions. There are photographs of some of the family at a black-tie event: my parents, Judy and Graham, Carol, Ann, Robin and me (see page 105). On other visits, Louise and I called out the bingo numbers, with a bit of help. Leyton had proved a friendly constituency since 1966 and my father was popular and it was an easy trip there from Hampstead Garden Suburb. It is now a desirable location for the young and trendy, but in those days it was essentially a working-class area of London.

No. 22 South Square now only had my parents there. On a holiday in Turkey, my father picked up an awful virus and was only saved by the American hospital in Ankara. My mother had to do all the nursing in the hospital, which was often customary in Turkey, and he was repatriated home. It was clear that the

My father sitting in a deckchair in the garden of 22 South Square, looking relaxed and with his ubiquitous pipe in hand, unlit

large house was no longer going to work for them, so the time was right to move on. They looked around at flats to buy, but in the end, in spring 1976, they took on a lease on a double-sized flat in Dolphin Square, Pimlico, at a very good price, which included heating and electricity – the heating then came off the outflow of hot water from Battersea Power Station across the river. The flat had two bedrooms, a sitting room, a study, a dining room and a kitchen and it worked very well. It was on the first floor and there was a lift, which was good for my father. There was a large central garden, where you could sit and read. There is a memorial bench to my father in these gardens. It was also very close to the Houses of Parliament and there was a car parking space. Dolphin Square was near some shops, but quiet and near the 24 bus and Pimlico Underground. The rent was paid from the proceeds of the sale of 22 South Square and my parents lived off interest on the capital from the sale of the house, and sometimes used up a bit of the capital too.

At South Square, there was an enormous amount of furniture and clothes from those who had lived in it over the years and had left behind, as there were so many rooms. My parents were not able to help, so it fell to Robin and me to clear everything up. We all took the furniture we wanted, but not all of us had the space to store or keep much. My father took the books he could fit

My mother dressed for electioneering with Carol's baby daughter Margaret, for the 1970 election

into the new study and dining room, with bookshelves also in the bedrooms, but many books had to be left behind; a collector came and took some, but there were hundreds over. There was a huge amount of stuff left. We bagged up what we could for charity and then it was left to the house clearers. The sale price for the house was not as much as it should have been, but my parents needed, for health reasons, to move out. Robin and I had lived there since we were two and it held many memories.

It was easy to visit my parents at Dolphin Square, though the flat was always hot. There was parking in the evenings and I often went to see them, sometimes with Louise. Robin was now back in London and could visit too. My mother had found a church in Pimlico called St Saviour's, very high church too, and we used to go with her if we were there on a Sunday. Father Geoffrey Pollard was a good vicar for the essentially aged congregation.

My father went into the Lords whenever Parliament was sitting. The Lords sittings used to end around 6.30 p.m., but those who had been in the Commons could stay on the green benches and in the bars and restaurants. My father would normally do this, playing chess and socialising and getting home when the Commons vote had been taken. Once he gave a lift to a fellow peer and invited him in for a drink. My mother said that it was terrible how hard they worked peers. He replied that the Lords only sat until around half-past six. Notwithstanding, my father continued to stay late whenever he could get away with it, spending time with friends and MPs.

Carol was greatly in love with David Brierley. He always wanted to write and left the advertising agency where he had worked since leaving Oxford and started writing thrillers at home, many of which were published, including some by me in paperback. In 1970, their daughter Margaret was born and there was a temporary separation. Carol and Margaret came to live with us at 22 South Square. They were soon happily reunited at their home in Kings Langley.

TWENTY-THREE

European Parliament: 1974–1975

The European Parliament initially had delegates appointed from all countries that were part of the community. My father was one of the first appointed members of the European Parliament, which ideally suited him and was a reward for loyalty and a perfect job in retirement. The position was not at this stage as onerous as it became when delegates were elected by party and major issues came under discussion. European parliamentarians did not have high salaries and perks, though bonafide expenses were covered. My father and my mother went to Brussels once a month and then to Strasbourg, where the whole operation transferred for one week in four. This was to placate the French, who opposed everything being in English and to this day, insist on dual translation in English and French, though far more people in the world speak or understand English better. They enjoyed their visits and my father was a passionate European. He told me that he particularly enjoyed the restaurants in Strasbourg. He knew many of the British delegates from all parties, most of whom had been in the Commons previously.

In the House of Lords, my father was still active with support for the Labour Party. He became associated with Ian Wrigglesworth's Manifesto Group and Bill Rodgers's Campaign for Labour Victory. His natural allies in the party were Roy Jenkins, Bill Rodgers, Shirley Williams and, perhaps less so, David Owen. He was a natural social democrat.

Harold Wilson suddenly resigned in March 1976 and there have been theories as to why this was, with it being suggested that he realised that he was suffering from early dementia. He

My father officially entering the House of Lords as a life peer, 1974, the year he stood down from the Commons

and my father had had a political marriage of convenience. He was succeeded by Jim Callaghan, but Labour had intractable problems with the trade unions, leading to the Winter of Discontent in 1978–1979, during which the streets became covered in rubbish and there was even talk of the dead not being buried, but this was hearsay. Labour always seemed to have financial problems when they took office and some believed that this was a result of Tory manipulation of the City, which was under their control. Callaghan continued in power until the very end of the term, in the hope of improvement in the polls, but in the end had to call an election.

In May 1979, Margaret Thatcher, who had succeeded Edward Heath in 1975, after he had lost the 1974 elections, won a majority of forty-three votes and Labour would be out of office until 1997. It was increasingly hard for Labour to lay a finger on Thatcher, though her policies were not popular, and they became increasingly desperate as to how to match her. In November 1980, Michael Foot was elected leader of the Labour Party, an event that astounded my father, just before his death, and marked the nadir for Labour – perhaps at least until Jeremy Corbyn came along. The donkey jacket that Foot wore at the Cenotaph will never be forgotten. Thatcher won a landslide in 1983, after the Falklands War the previous year, and then cemented her position in 1987. Faced with such a fate for the Labour Party, it is possible that my father would have found a home with the SDP, but we will never know. It is the only political party that I ever joined and I still have my membership card as a memento.

TWENTY-FOUR

Family: 1976–1980

In 1976, after five years together, Louise and I were married, the last in the family, at the Chapel of the Royal Hospital with a guard of honour of Chelsea pensioners, resplendent in their red tunics. Louise's father was a commissioner there, having been a distinguished soldier, with an impressive war record and rising to the rank of general. He must have been surprised by Louise's socialising in the Leyton constituency. My friend John Heskett was best man and made a very witty speech. We started married life in a nice small Fulham house and I used to bring my parents to Sunday lunch there. Our first child, Tom, was born on 2 September 1978 and Emily was born on 11 November 1981, after my father had died.

My father with Tom aged 2, just before my father died

My father with his eldest grandchild, Margaret, Carol's daughter. She is giving him a drink. It shows his love for small children

My father loved small children and he knew four of his grandchildren. There was our Tom – there is a photo of my father holding Tom's hand, aged two, and walking with his inevitable stick; Carol's daughter Margaret Brierley, who appears in a photo taken while they were temporarily at South Square being carried by my mother, who wears a red dress and a red rosette for the 1970 election; and Robin's children, Patrick and Anna. Patrick used to be dropped off at Dolphin Square while their mother June went to her job as a teacher. We would sit with my father in the garden of Dolphin Square, watching the select world go by.

Judy and Graham were still together, but more distant from each other. The lived in Walton Street and had a lovely country house in Wotton Underwood, Buckinghamshire, which had been the old dairy – the big house, built for the 2nd Duke of Buckingham, and is now lived in by Tony Blair. For Judy's birthday, Graham had bought her a Mini Moke, a trendy open-framed car with a tarpaulin cover, and asked me to collect it and drive it to Wotton and put it in the garage as a surprise for her. This I did, but I cannot now remember how I got back. Graham had been born to rule, and like many Etonians, had a sense of entitlement. Although he scarcely helped me in our shared career in publishing, I always tended to do what he asked.

When they finally split up – they were divorced in 1976 – they still remained friends. Judy embarked on a wild period and eventually she crashed the Mini Moke when under the influence, though this was hushed up. Graham called on me again and told me what had happened and we were all worried that Judy might be in a bad way, as the car was open on all sides – I don't think there were even seat belts. Judy was all right, miraculously, and Graham asked me to get the car towed away from the roadside, in a street in Kilburn: The car was a total wreck and I could not believe that anybody could have survived, but she did.

TWENTY-FIVE

Death: 2 December 1980

My father's health never fully recovered from the virus he picked up on holiday in Turkey, when his life was saved by the American hospital and by my mother's determination and assistance, nor from his hip operation. Dolphin Square was perfect for him, being warm and a taxi ride from the Houses of Parliament, for he had given up driving. He looked older than he was and spent his time reading, doing the crossword and watching sport. I have often thought what would have happened if he could have subscribed to Sky Sports – not in operation then – bearing in mind his dislike for Rupert Murdoch and any press baron: he was a loyal BBC man. I think a compromise would have been reached whereby his children gave him a Sky subscription as a birthday present, so that he could have watched it all the time, but without having passed any money on directly to its proprietor.

My father had become increasingly out of breath, even when just sitting. I was really worried when at a lunch with Andrew Rudolf and his family, he started breathing very heavily. Bearing in mind the weak male Gordon Walker hearts, it was a real concern. He continued to go into the House of Lords and eased up a bit, although he was not aware that anything was really wrong and he was not observant at this stage. He was increasingly sedentary, watching TV most of the time. I made a point of seeing him as much as I could.

On 2 December 1980, his taxi drew up at the entrance of the House of Lords and he was found to be dead on arrival. Black Rod was summoned and the taxi drove to the nearby Westminster Hospital. I was later to meet the then Black Rod, David Stileman, at a church we both attended in Wimbledon. We talked about the tragedy and we thanked him. It was fortunate that such a devout and caring man was the first person to tell my mother what had happened.

I was at work and out of the office when my mother rang with the news, leaving a message with one of my team, who had to tell me the news, in tears. I rushed to Dolphin Square, where family members gathered. My mother was not surprisingly distraught and not really taking anything in. As my father had died away from home, a poor policeman, looking very young, had been sent to break the news and was very relieved when he found out that we knew already. The family all gathered around, but it was less of a shock for those who regularly saw him, as they knew that he did not have long to live, even though he was only a few months over seventy-three.

My mother never got over this last tragedy and I think saw her life being full of so many disappointments: her Oxford degree, the loss of her war work, Smethwick, Leyton and finally my father's death at a relatively young age – she was to be a widow for twenty-five years. All her life she had found solace in the church and St Saviour's in Pimlico became even more important to her.

There were soon hundreds of letters of condolence, including a telegram from the Queen and Prince Philip as my father was a member of the Privy Council and a companion of honour. I registered the death and then we planned the funeral, which took place on Monday 8 December 1980 at St Saviour's. The church was packed and Robin and I read lessons and Father Geoffrey Pollard gave the address.

As my mother was coping with grief and despair, she had a letter from the Home Office, saying that as she had been born in Jamaica, she had only had a right to residence in the UK through her husband, born in Worthing, and now that he had died, she had to go back home, despite having been in the country for nearly fifty years. It was an unwelcome distraction and knocked her back further. With help from some MPs and representations by the family, including advice from Graham Greene, the decision was reversed and all was well – but it showed what some people, with less influence, had to go through.

There was a movement for a memorial service, which would have been right and suitable for my father, at St Margaret's, Westminster and we moved towards planning for it. My mother, however, was not really up to it and worried about money, though there was ample available. She was now very nervous and found almost everything alarmed her. We went along with her wishes, but in retrospect we should, as a family, have overruled my mother and arranged a fitting memorial for my father.

She had coped with coming from Jamaica aged eighteen, she had supported my father at Oxford and in the war and then in his political career. Just as she was to be a companion to the foreign secretary this was taken from her, at Smethwick and then Leyton. She had nursed my father through illness and now he was gone. All these losses were not her fault, but she had suffered through disasters that she had no control over. She was never fully to recover her equilibrium and tended, not surprisingly, to see the worst of most occasions.

There were obituaries and tributes. The gist of these was that my father had been a great politician, achieving much, but was an unlucky one. He bore his disappointments with courage and fortitude. He was seen as being somewhat out of touch with modern politics and modern ways. It was hinted, for example, that he would never have shortened his name to Pat Walker, and I am not sure if it would have made much difference to his performance or luck. He never built up a following among Labour members and was not a charismatic speaker. George Brown was the complete opposite, but he did not rise much higher. In some ways, it was suggested, he was in the wrong party, but he could never have been a Conservative. If he had held Leyton in the by-election, one could see him as staying as foreign secretary for several years. It was the job for him, full of intelligent people, with opportunities to travel to America and around the Commonwealth. It was a big department, but not a spending department, unlike Education, where he had the misfortune to take over just after the pound had been devalued and savage costs had to be made.

In some ways he seemed the academic he was, but we were proud of what he achieved. Napoleon wanted lucky generals and I am afraid my father was not lucky, from elections in Oxford, to Smethwick and Leyton. The newspapers never printed pictures of him smiling, but he was an amusing man and could give witty impromptu speeches, which always ended with a joke, which reminds me of… Most of these now would be considered politically incorrect, though they were always pretty innocent.

He was a wonderful father, warm, witty, confident, and a friend to all his family and to many others. We loved him and it was a great shock and a deep loss when he was no longer with us. I still miss him and think of him often and wish he had had a chance to see our children, and all his grandchildren, grow up.

TWENTY-SIX

The Family: 1980–2005

My mother stayed in Dolphin Square and became increasingly worried, lonely and defeated by the death of her husband. The family did what they could to help and we felt the need to spend as much time as we could with her, often taking her to St Saviour's Church and inviting her for Sunday lunch. Carol and David had moved to France to the Dordogne, Ann was in Madison, Wisconsin, and Judy and my mother did not really get on – a hangover from the evacuation to Jamaica in the war. Looking after her fell to Robin and me, and mainly to me and Louise. Her isolation and sense of fear increased over the years and we comforted her as much as we could.

My parents and all of us in the UK would go to Carol and David on Boxing Day and Ann and Andy would come when they were in the country. Although Ann had two daughters – Jenny, born in 1974 in the UK and Kate, born in 1976 – they were essentially in America, so hardly saw my father. Robin married his second wife, Magally, in 1987 and had Alex the same year, so sadly they did not meet my father.

My mother either came to us in our lovely Fulham house or we to her. In 1987, we went to live in Sydney for a posting when I took over as managing director of Hodder & Stoughton, having loved the country on previous visits, and my mother came for quite a long stay. We had rented a lovely house and there was a guest room for her. She had relations and friends, some from Jamaica who were also distant cousins of Louise. I took her to Canberra, where she had been when my father was at the Commonwealth Office.

When Tom was about eleven, in 1989, he was at the junior school of King's College, Wimbledon. We were not sure if he would pass into the senior school, where the intake was tough and competitive. We looked around at alternative schools, but there was nothing of the same standard. Neither Louise nor I had liked boarding school and we chose London day schools for Tom and Emily. Something made me consider Wellington as a back-up and we went to look at it. It still all seemed so familiar that a bout of nostalgia hit me. Tom saw the headmaster with us, and we decided, with powerful help from Louise, that it was not for us. In the event, Tom sailed into the senior school and was a great success academically and at sport. Emily went to Putney High and also achieved great success there.

Much later, around 2014, I became involved with publishing two books about Wellington: *Path of Duty* by my Uncle Robin, a thinly disguised account of how he had come to leave in support of the chaplain in the war years; and *Out of Bounds*, about the Romilly brothers, Giles and Esmond, who while at Wellington produced a left-wing magazine. Esmond left and Giles stayed on. Esmond fought in the Spanish Civil War and eloped with Decca Mitford, one of the notorious Mitford girls. Wellington decided to run a symposium on these two books and Robin and I went back and spoke about both of them – quite a few copies were bought. We returned once more, for a reception for those who had gone up in our year, but otherwise we had little contact with the school. We made few friends there and many of the OWs we knew later were ones we had not known while we were there.

Judy eventually found great happiness with Norman Gowar, whom she married in 1981. He had two lovely children, Kate and Matthew, quite young then. Judy was a wonderful stepmother, known as Didi – after our grandmother – to them and their children.

Robin found happiness with his second wife, Magally, and they had Alex together, to add to Patrick and Anna by his first marriage. Magally was a loving stepmother to Patrick and Anna and their families. Robin's first wife, June, married John Izbicki in October 1986. He was an education correspondent on the *Telegraph*, who came to press conferences during my brief spell on the education side of Hodder & Stoughton in the early 1970s. John moved to Paris with the *Telegraph*, with June and Patrick and Anna. He was a loving stepfather, and I published his autobiography, *Life Between the Lines*, in 2012. It did very well and we became firm friends, having lovely lunches near Waterloo station, at his favourite Turkish restaurant, to discuss the progress of the book. He sadly died in December 2020, aged ninety-one, and his funeral was packed, despite Covid restrictions. There were several moving tributes and obituaries.

Ann and Andy split up and their two children were basically with Ann, visiting Andy, who had moved to a university in Alabama, with Gail, who became his second wife. Ann stayed in Madison and kept the family house, which had been purchased mostly with a gift from my parents. She went on working in the lab as a senior administrator, as well as looking after Jenny and Kate. She loved living in Madison, a charming and special town revolving around the university. Like much of Wisconsin, it was built on a series of lakes.

Carol had always been very religious, like our mother, first at the church in Kings Langley, where she was a churchwarden, and then in Belvès when they moved to the Dordogne. Margaret stayed in the UK to study and lodged with Judy and Norman. Carol became a lay reader in a series of redundant Catholic churches which could be used for Anglican services. She had not driven for many years but had to start again as her house was so isolated and the parish so large. The chaplain in Bordeaux covered so many parishes that he could only come one Sunday a month. The marriage eventually ended and David eventually found a new partner and they were subsequently married, leaving the house for Carol, which had been bought also with help from my parents. On her own, she decided that now was the time to train to be a priest. Carol came back to Durham for a year – because she had read Greek at university and was of a certain age, she could study for only a year – and we saw her occasionally in this time. She was made a deacon in a service in Berne in Switzerland,

Family photo to celebrate my mother's 90th birthday, at our house, Sunday 23 December 2001, the day before her actual birthday. Front row, from left *Anna and Patrick (Robin's children) Emily, our daughter, and Kate and her sister Jenny, in white (Ann's children), Alex, Robin's son with Magally, Carol.* Back row *Kate and Matthew Gowar, Norman's children, Magally, Margaret, Carol's daughter, Ann, my mother, Judy with Robin and behind, Louise with Norman. At the very back are our son Tom and me with a bow tie*

to which her daughter Margaret and I went. The Bishop of Gibraltar in Europe would ordain a deacon, but did not believe in ordaining women priests, so she had to be ordained by an archbishop and the service was held in Canterbury – rather than in her parish-to-be in France – by the Archbishop of Canterbury in September 2003, which we all attended. She went back to France as a fully fledged priest.

All this slightly washed over my mother. It did not help that she had been brought up to disapprove of women priests and never changed her views to accommodate her daughter. Carol was mainly in France anyway, where we went to see her back in the Dordogne. The church was, and always had been, my mother's mainstay. Andrew Rudolf would come and visit. He had married Juliet and had three children, Sophie, Jessica and Christian. He was always concerned to help my mother and he and Juliet came to visit when they could.

My mother became increasingly anxious as time went on, and we had to visit more and more often, which fell to Robin and me, though we were both working, Robin as a civil servant and me as a publisher. In 1989, I came back early from Australia to take up a new job, while the rest of the family stayed in Australia to complete the school year. Our house was let out, so I stayed in Dolphin Square for three months in my father's bedroom. It was a curious time. She did not initially want to give me a key and worried if I was not back early. I was working very hard, having to socialise, but she ideally wanted me to be there all the time. Somehow, we survived and it meant that she had company and the other members of the family did not have to worry. Carol would also stay when she was back from France seeing her daughter Margaret and friends. Ann would visit occasionally, sometimes with Jenny and Kate, and before my father died my parents went out once to see her in Madison.

Our children, Tom and Emily, went to day school where they were both great successes and both went on to the University of Edinburgh.

In the 1990s, my mother remained at Dolphin Square. She donated a splendid portrait of my father to the National Portrait Gallery, without any of the family knowing. It has only been on display once when there was an exhibition on politicians. Otherwise, it lives in the vaults. We have twice tried to buy it back, but they will not sell, so we only have small reproductions of it in black and white. (I managed to license a colour version, which is on the front cover of this book.) My mother was visited by the increasing family. Patrick was fifteen, Anna thirteen, and they saw my mother with Robin and Magally, who was fond of my mother, especially as most of her family were in Venezuela and so she identified with being far away from family, as my mother had done. Margaret was twenty and away at university and our children were twelve and nine. They would visit with Louise and me, or my mother would come to us, now in Putney. Judy would be an occasional visitor. St Saviour's Church was my mother's main social meeting place and she got to know the congregation and was cared for by Father Pollard and his team. She also had an excellent GP practice nearby and went to the shops in Tachbrook Street. She was still quite mobile and liked to get out of the flat.

I seemed to drive her to several funerals of friends of her age. There was a full Requiem Mass in the Suburb for Sarah Collins, the widow of Norman Collins, who had started ATV with Lew Grade. The mass was to my mother's liking. We went down to Kent for the funeral of Elspeth Skilbeck, the widow of my father's oldest friend, Dunstan (Dustpan), and there were others. It helped for her to go with someone and of course she no longer drove or had a car.

My mother was getting increasingly absent minded and Robin and I became more concerned about her living on her own. We took her to the doctor for a test on memory, assuming that she would fail, but a sudden lucidity meant that she could give her address – which she couldn't normally – and say who the prime minister was – a lucky guess, but she passed and was allowed to stay living independently. Fortunately, in those days there were porters in each of the blocks in Dolphin Square, and the one in Frobisher House was particularly helpful. He kept an eye out for her and had Robin's and my contact details. Through this help, she was able to carry on living in the Square. (The porters have long gone.)

Then she started to think that people on the television were real and would ring at all hours to say that there were people in the house and we had to reassure her. By the late 1990s, she was going to the church instead of the surgery and vice versa, and again the porters were able to warn us, but it was not long before she would need to have someone in the house to look after her and to help her. We put it off as long as we could, but eventually the time came. I made enquiries and found two people who could live in for alternate weeks. It was quite a nightmare, as I had to get all the food, pay them in cash and hear all their tales of woe.

With the rent to pay, it was expensive too. My mother hated it, but the porters could no longer cope with her wanderings.

This arrangement lasted about a year and then my mother had a fall. The carer was unable to lift her on her own and I went round to help. Most people who could no longer cope living on their own in Dolphin Square went to St George's nursing home in the nearby St George's Square. My sister Judy checked that there was a room and we wheeled her in her wheelchair straight to the home, where she could be looked after with more staff and meals provided. I paid off the carers with relief and now we knew that she was safe. It was not as expensive as some homes, nor as smart, but it suited her. It had a religious feel to it and the matron and others dressed as nuns, which is how she had been brought up and the same as in her Oxford days. There was a Catholic priest in the home and my mother went to mass every morning. She had always gone to high Anglican churches, so she could scarcely tell the difference.

She became more and more confused and her short-term memory began to disappear. I visited in the week – I was now working as a freelance so could choose my time more carefully – and Robin would come on Sunday and take her across the road to St Saviour's, a couple of minutes away. She had lucid moments and then the clouds gathered again. Often, she asked me who my favourite child was and I said both of them: this could not be possible for her. She was clearly remembering that Neville had been her mother's favourite, not her. It must have still hurt, all those decades before.

She broke a hip and was taken to St Thomas' Hospital and was through casualty before I could get there. She was able to go home quite soon as there was the nursing staff to look after her. She later broke her other hip, falling out of bed, and again was seen quickly, but she was then in a Catch-22 situation. The hospital said they would not release her until she had done her exercises. She did not understand what they meant and could not do the exercises anyway. I had to get the matron from the home to come and explain the position and that she was well cared for. Eventually they let her leave. She was not happy in the home and could be quite tart with the staff. Maybe she was remembering putting her mother into a home when Didi was old and infirm.

In 2004, my mother went downhill. She talked, but it now made no sense, she could remember nothing and she lived in a state of panic, as if she was always doing something wrong and some disaster was to befall her. I think that this was the cumulative effect of all the misfortunes that she had experienced, coming back through her unconscious. She was well cared for and fed, but her quality of life was pretty grim. Going to St Saviour's was one of the few high points for her, pushed in a wheelchair. As the year went on, she gradually got worse and slowly stopped eating. In late 2004, we were summoned by the nursing home and told to assume the worst, but not immediately. We gathered again in early 2005, except for Ann, who was in Wisconsin, and the Jamaican nurse who sat with those near death said on 3 January that she would last the night. She did and died on the early morning of 4 January 2005, peacefully in her sleep.

In many ways it was a blessed release for her, because her life had no high points and only low. We arranged the funeral for 19 January – January is a month of many deaths, and this was the earliest that it could be take place. St Saviour's was full of family, old friends, neighbours from Dolphin Square and the Suburb and some of those who had known my father. Ann, Robin and I gave readings from the Bible, and Judy read an epitaph by Sir Walter Raleigh. Carol gave a blessing and the address was by Andrew Rudolf, my mother's paternal cousin, who summed her up very well: they went back a long way. There were refreshments in the church rooms and then a private cremation. There were letters of condolence from the many people who were touched by her life of generosity and help for those in need, from Oxford days, to inviting one and all to stay, helping those who came from Hampton School in Jamaica to the UK and keeping the family and cousins together. Both our parents were now gone.

TWENTY-SEVEN

Family Updated: 2005–2022

This is an attempt to bring the story up to date. There were births, divorces and deaths – hatches, matches and despatches. My eldest sister Judith married Norman Gowar in 1981. He was vice chancellor of Royal Holloway College and Judy was a professor at the Open University and the author of erudite books on linguistics. They lived first in Islington, then moved to a lovely house in Luckhurst in Kent with a big garden, where the family was often invited. After this, they returned to Islington to an elegant house in Prior Bolton Street. It was there that Judy suffered a stroke, from which she tragically never recovered: she died on 24 April 2016, aged just 89, after she and Norman had had thirty-five very happy years together. There was a moving ceremony at Golders Green crematorium. Norman's daughter Kate, born in 1967, has two children with her then partner Rich: Florence (Flossie) (2006) and Martha (2008). Norman's son Matthew was born in 1969 and married Paula in 2002 and they have a daughter Farrah (2004) and a son Caspar (2007). Norman has remained close friends with Judy's family, and it is always a pleasure to see him. He still lives in Islington: and I miss our pre-pandemic visits to Tate Modern.

Carol came back from France to live in the UK, having found it increasingly difficult to live on her own in a remote location. She also found driving long journeys to neighbouring churches for services a concern. Another factor was that when she had first helped as a lay reader, before ordination, there had been few to help. By the end of her time in the Dordogne, so many priests had retired that she was not in the same demand as previously. Margaret, born in 1970 and Chris Johnson, born in 1951 developed a house in Brighton with a granny flat for Carol and they lived happily together there. Margaret and Chris had two sons: Robin (2004) and Luke (2006). They married in 2016 and Chris sadly died in 2017. Initially Carol lived independently and helped in nearby churches in Brighton, particularly one where the vicar welcomed women priests. The then Bishop of Chichester, who was responsible for the Brighton area, was against women clergy, which limited her choice of churches. After some years sharing together, Carol became more and more confused and eventually she had to move into a nursing home in Brighton, initially to an independent flat and then to a room in the infirmary. When it suddenly closed, Carol moved to a Christian care home in Worthing, where the continuity of staff has meant there have been no outbreaks of Covid-19. She is well looked after, and we are now allowed to visit.

Ann had lived for many decades in Madison, Wisconsin and very sadly died there on 27 January 2021, aged 76, from cancer of the oesophagus which spread to her liver. I went out to see her in early 2020 before the cancer had spread and spent ten days with her. We could not attend her funeral because of the pandemic, but it was streamed on zoom and over twenty of the family in the UK joined in. Ann's eldest daughter Jenny was born in 1974 and married Timothy Truitt in 1998 and they have a daughter Cassie (2003) and a son Quintin (2006). They live in Virginia. Kate, Ann's younger daughter was born in 1976 and married Alex Lemuz in 2003 and they were divorced in 2016. Their children are a daughter Scarlett (2005), a son Dominic (2008) and a second son Logan (2011). Kate and the children live in Oregon.

Our son Tom, born in 1978, married Helen Boyle in July 2016 in a church wedding in Ledbury, Herefordshire, followed by a stunning marquee reception in her parent's garden. They have a daughter Maya (August 2017) and a son Max (March 2019). They live in a beautifully converted stable next door to us. Our daughter Emily, born in 1981, married Alexander Gilmour in February 2013 in the Temple Church with a fabulous reception afterwards at St John Restaurant in Smithfield. Their son Rufus Gordon Gilmour was born November 2017, and they live in Hackney. We have lived in the same family house in Roehampton for thirty years: we are fortunate to see Tom and family nearly every day. Emily and her family come as often as they can, and we and the cousins look forward to these times together. Tom is deputy head of an Academy school in Ham, Richmond and Emily is a barrister and an employment judge.

My brother Robin married June Barr in 1974 and their son Patrick was born in 1976 and their daughter Anna in 1977. We would see them there until they were divorced in 1984, when June married John Izbicki and the children were living with them in France. Patrick married Mary Ward in July 1979 and they have a daughter Robyn (2010) and a son Daniel (2012). They live in Eire and Patrick watches English football and cricket with equal enthusiasm: we often meet at Lords. Anna married Stefan Ivanovitch in a ceremony in France in May 2014. They have twin sons, Arthur (Artie) and Luke, (2018) and they live in Greenwich. Robin married Magally Flores in 1987, which we sadly missed as we were in Australia. Their son was born in the same year and Robin and Magally had a wonderful and happy marriage for nearly thirty years. This marriage came to a tragic end in 2016 when Robin died of heart failure, aged only 69. There was a moving service in a church in Dulwich which was packed full. I gave the main address and knew, in practising it, the exact moment I would crack up, which proved to be the case on the day. There was a reception afterwards. Magally and Alex still live in East Dulwich, and we see Magally as often as we can and Alex often at Lords with Patrick.

Graham Greene, Judy's first husband, born in 1936, died in October 2016, aged 80, with many obituaries and tributes. Andrew Rudolf was born in 1937 and his wife Juliet in 1938.They were married in 1966 and had over fifty years of happy and fulfilled marriage, until Juliet's untimely death on 18 March 2018. We see Andrew from time to time, sadly limited by the pandemic. Andrew and Juliet had a daughter Sophie (1968) and a daughter Jessica (1969), who with her husband Mark has five children. Their son Christian (1974) is my godson.

The members of the family of all generations met as often as they could. Robin and Magally went to Venezuela to see her extended family, and they have a timeshare in Wales where their family still all meet together, very sadly now without Robin. Judy and Norman went on trips together and Ann came over to the UK regularly. Louise and I, often with our children, went on visits to Australia, India and Sri Lanka. We also spent much time in Louise's family cottage in Polruan, including five months in lockdown in 2020. The cottage was sadly sold in June 2021, but we return regularly through the generosity of friends. Emily and Al now have a cottage in Norfolk, where we see them and Rufus.

* * *

Carol and I are the only ones left out of the five children, which is why I wanted now to put straight the story of my father Patrick, my mother Audrey and the whole family. Most importantly, as my father did not write an autobiography, this is, I hope, the next best thing.

AFTERWORD

The Extended Gordon Walker Family

The family tree on pages x-xi shows many cousins and Gordon Walker relations for my father. The key part of his family is often mentioned in the text, but below is a summary of the others who bear the Gordon Walker name.

My father's cousins James (Jim) and Brian Thomas Gordon-Walker, both sons of Robin Ernest, my father's uncle, were schoolteachers. Jim was a Catholic, married first to Cecily Cummings, and had one child by her – John Patrick, born in 1947. He stayed with us in South Square when he was at university in London. Cecily sadly died in 1956 but in 1959 Jim married Elizabeth Granville, with whom he had four children. John Patrick married Sally Grant in 1972 and their children were Lorna, born 1975, Timothy Thomas, born 1978, and Emma, born 1981. The trouble was that Jim was fond of the demon drink, and the proceeds of several schools disappeared into off-licences. The Catholic church was a great support to him in time of troubles, especially when his first wife died. Brian also bailed him out, but the assumption was that the Patrick Gordon Walker family must be rolling in money and Jim would not believe that our family was living on a small political salary and the support of my father's mother. My parents did what they could to help, but it was never enough for Cecily.

We did meet the children of the second marriage. Simon, born 1960, kept up with my brother Robin and my mother when she was widowed, who helped him with university fees – a way of making up for what we had not been able to give his father Jim: my brother was nervous that our inheritance was going to Simon.

Simon married Yvonne McAllen and they had two sons, James, born in 1994, and Daniel, born in 1996 (Simon sadly died in 2018, aged only fifty-eight – the dreaded GW heart striking again). Rupert, a keen cricketer, born in 1961, came to see us when we lived in Sydney and he was on a cricket tour of Australia. He did not marry. I only met Julian at Simon's funeral. He was born in 1962 and married in 1989 Joanne Britton and they had one son, Dominic, born in 1996. Sarah, the youngest and only daughter, was born in 1966 and joined the law firm used by the publishing company that I then worked for. When I went to a meeting there, the solicitor produced a young trainee to take notes, and enjoyed introducing me to Sarah. When she lived near us in London, I met up with her occasionally for dog walks. She married in 1988 Robert Crossley and had Florence, born in 2000, Rose, born in 2002, and Dulcie, born in 2005. Jim died in 1989, aged 76.

Brian Thomas in the end abandoned his brother Jim and set up a school of his own. He married Joyce Patrick in 1938, to whose funeral I went with my mother. They had a son Robert (Bob), born in 1939; he married Janet Smith in 1966, and they had two sons, Lee Thomas, born in 1970, and Scott, born in 1974. Brian also had a daughter, Jenny, born in 1945, who had a son, another Patrick. We met her and her family when they lived in Wimbledon. By her second marriage to John Naylor in 1973, she had Alexander, born 1975, and Arabella, born 1979.

Bob Gordon Walker and his children Lee and Scott found in the end that the land that the school was on in East Grinstead was far more valuable for building houses on than for running a school, so they sold the land, the school closed, and their family received a large windfall. Brian died in 1979, aged sixty-five.

APPENDIX

Belsen Diaries

The extracts below about my father's April 1945 visit to Belsen with a BBC radio recording car come from the contemporaneous diaries he kept. The first two parts of the diaries appeared in his book *The Lid Lifts*, published in 1945 by Victor Gollancz. The last part of the diaries extracted below is headed 'April 1945: Reflections on Belsen' and comes from the subsequent publication of his *Political Diaries, 1932–1971*. It was not included in either his radio broadcast or *The Lid Lifts*. Both of these excised any mention of anti-Russian or personal comments, which were not felt to be suitable.

The 'Reflections on Belsen' make powerful reading about the evils of the concentration camps, with a taster extract below:

> For here we are face to face with evil ... [C]amps like Belsen and Buchenwald [are a] deliberate, coldly calculated and coolly executed assault on the very foundation of our Western life – which is the respect of individual human life, the distinction between the human and the animal.

20 April 1945

Drove to Celle. Through pine and birch country. Bridges down all over the place over the canal outside Brunswick. We had to make a big detour eastwards (towards the German pocket) to find a bridge. Masses of foreign workers still on the road. We saw one cartload of Italians driving two sleek little Shetland ponies. Celle is a beautiful old, undamaged town.

Got to Belsen. It is a vast area surrounded by barbed wire. The whole thing was being guarded by armed Hungarian guards. They had been in the German army and are now, immediately and without hesitation, serving us. They are saving us a large number of men for the time being, guarding the camp outside, every 20 yards or so, day and night. Outside the camp which is amidst birches, pines and heath – all fairly recently planted – were great notices in red letters – **'Danger Typhus'**. We drove into what turned out to be a great training camp – a sort of Aldershot. Fine two-storey buildings, brick, with asphalt roads – Adolf Hitler Strasse, Rommel Strasse, Fredericus Rex Strasse, etc. A fine officers' house at the end to which we drove and where we found officers of the Oxfordshire Yeomanry. Colonel Taylor in command was a pupil of mine at Oxford. They made us welcome and we had a drink with them.

They began to tell us about the Concentration Camp. It lies south of the training area: it is behind its own barbed wire. The Wehrmacht was not allowed near it. It was guarded entirely by SS-men and women.

This is what I discovered about the relief of the camp, which happened on the 15th. I got this story from Derek Sington and officers and men of the Oxfordshire Yeomanry.

Typhus broke out in the camp and a truce was arranged so that we could take the camp over. The Germans originally proposed that we should by-pass the camp. In the meanwhile thousands and thousands of people would have died and been shot. We refused these terms and demanded the withdrawal of the Germans and the disarmament of the SS guards.

Some dozen SS men and women were left behind under the command of Hauptsturmfuehrer Kramer – who had been at Auschwitz. Apparently they had been told all sorts of fairy-tales about the truce: that they could go on guarding – that we would let them free, etc. In fact all that had been agreed was that the camp should for a few days be a neutral zone so that we could take over and prevent the inmates breaking out and spreading typhus.

Sington (who has done a magnificent job of work) arrived with a few trucks and was met by Kramer who showed them round the camp. There were volleys of cheers all the way – people broke out of the compounds to greet the British spearhead.

Kramer seemed to expect us to accept his attitude as quite normal. He did not expect us to be shocked by the things we saw. He had been the man who stood by the ovens at Auschwitz and picked out those to be burned at once. He described the inmates of the camp as *asozial* – anti-social, useless people. He clearly regarded them as cattle. As our men drove in, the SS opened fire from their towers on people who broke out of a compound to get at a potato field. This was stopped quickly. We only had a handful of men so far and the SS stayed there that night. The first night of liberty many hundreds of people died of joy.

Next day some men of the Oxfordshire Yeomanry arrived. People crowded round them kissing their hands and feet and dying from weakness. Corpses in every stage of decay were lying around, piled up on top of each other in heaps. There were corpses in the compounds, in the blocks. People were falling dead all around, people who were walking skeletons. One woman came up to the soldier who was guarding the milk-store and doling milk out to children and begged for milk for her baby. The man took the baby and saw it had been dead for days – black in the face and shrivelled up. The mother went on begging for milk – so he poured some into its dead lips. The mother than gibbered and crooned with joy (the soldier's own words) – and carried the baby off in triumph. She stumbled and fell dead in a few yards. Another soldier told how they had come across an Englishman, just moving amongst the corpses. He had enough strength to say he was English. They lifted him up, put him in a jeep and took him away. Outside the camp he said: 'Now I can die in peace. I am outside the camp. I don't want to smoke; I don't want to eat; I don't want to drink. I want to die in peace.' I have these stories and some others on records spoken by the men who saw them.

On [the] 16th Kramer and the SS were arrested and were very heavily beaten up by our men with boots and rifle butts. Kramer was taken off and kept in a cold larder (with some stinking fish) of the officers' home. He has now gone back to rear. The rest, men and women, were kept under guard (to save them from the inmates). They were set to work shovelling up the corpses into lorries. 35,000 corpses are reckoned – more actually than the living, about 30,000.

The SS men were driven and pushed along and made to ride on top of the loaded corpses and then shovel them into the great mass open graves. They were so tired and beaten up that they fell exhausted among the corpses. (I saw this myself later.) Jeering crowds collected around them and they had to be kept under strong guard. One man committed suicide and one attempted suicide in their cells. Two jumped off the lorries and tried to run away and get lost in the crowds. They were shot down. One jumped into a concrete pool of water and was riddled with bullets. The other was brought to the ground with a shot in the belly and was then finished off with a sten-gun.

The SS women are made to cook and carry heavy loads. One of them tried to commit suicide. The inmates say that they were more cruel and brutal than the men. They are all young – in their 20s. One SS woman tried to hide, disguised as a prisoner. She was denounced and arrested.

The camp was so full because people had been brought here from East and West. Some people were brought here from Nordhausen, 5 days' journey without food. Many had marched for 2–3 days. There was no food at all in the camp. A few piles of mangold-wurzels amidst the piles of dead bodies. Some of the dead bodies were of people so hungry that, though the mangold-wurzels were guarded by SS men, they had tried to storm them and been shot down then and there. There was no water. Nothing but these wurzels and some boiled stinking carrots – enough for a few hundred people. Men and women had fought for raw mangold-wurzels. Dead bodies – black and blue and bloated – and skeletons had been used as pillows by sick people.

The day after we took over 7 *Blockleiter* – mostly Poles – were murdered by the inmates. Some were still beating the people. We arrested one woman who had beaten another with a board. She admitted quite frankly to the offence. We are arresting these people.

An enormous dump of personal jewellery and belongings was discovered – in suitcases.

When I went into the camp five days after its liberation there were still bodies all around. I saw about a thousand – perhaps two thousand. In one place hundreds had been shovelled into a mass grave by bulldozers. In another Hungarian soldiers were putting corpses into a grave that was 60 feet by 60 feet and 20 feet deep. It was almost half-full. Other similar pits were being dug. 5,000 people had died since we got into the camp. People died before my eyes – scarcely human moaning skeletons, many of them gone mad. Bodies were just piled up, higgledy-piggledy in piles. Many had gashed wounds and bullet marks and terrible sores. One Englishman (who had lived in Ostend) was picked up half-dead. It was found that he had a great bullet wound in his back. He could just speak. He had no idea when he had been shot. He must have been lying half-conscious when some SS men shot him as he was crawling about. This was quite common.

I walked all round the camp. Everywhere the smell and odour of death. After a few hours you get used to it and don't notice it any more. People have typhus and dysentery. At one compound I went into I saw women standing up quite naked washing themselves; nearby were piles of corpses; other women, suffering from dysentery, were defecating in the open and then staggering back, half-dead to their blocks. Some were lying groaning on the ground. Life has reverted to the absolute primitive.

A great job has been done in getting water into the camp. It has been pumped in from outside and carried by hoses all over the camp, with frequent outlet points. There are taps of fresh clean water everywhere. Carts with water move around. The RASC [Royal Army Service Corps] has also done a great job in getting food in.

I went into the typhus ward – packed thick with people lying in dirty rags and blankets on the floor, groaning and moaning. By the door sat an English Tommy – talking to the people and cheering them up, though they couldn't understand what he said – and ladling milk out of a cauldron.

I collected together some women who could speak English and German and began to make records. An amazing thing is the number who have managed to keep themselves clean and neat. All of them said that in a day or two more they would have gone under from hunger and weakness. There are three main classes in the camp: the healthy who have managed to keep themselves decent – nearly all have had typhus. Then there are the sick, who are more or less cared for by their friends. Then there is the vast underworld that have lost all self-respect, crawling around in rags, living in abominable squalor, defecating in the compounds, often mad or half-mad. By the other prisoners they are called the Mussulmen. It is these who are still dying like flies. They can hardly walk on their legs. Thousands still of these cannot be saved – and if they were, would be useless lunatic invalids for the short remainder of their pitiful lives.

There are a very large number of girls in the camp, mostly Jewesses from Auschwitz. They have to be healthy to have survived. Over and over again I was told the same story – of the parades at which people stood naked for hours and were picked out arbitrarily (allegedly incapable of work) for the gas chambers and crematoriums, where many were burnt alive. Only a person in perfect health survived. Life and death was a question of pure chance. I talked to two pretty sisters – Anita and Renate Lasker, nieces of Lasker the chess player. Renate had nearly died of typhus at Auschwitz. The inspection was made. Everyone was told to stand up – those who could not were written down on the death list. Renate could not stand. Her name was written down: she said 'I'm the sister of one of the girls who play in the Orchestra.' 'Oh, that's all right then.' And her name was crossed off. Otherwise she would have been dead in a few hours. Only those who played in the orchestra or did some similar work had some chance to survive.

At Auschwitz the band was made to play at the station as the new batches of inmates arrived and during the parades when those to be gassed and burned were picked out. At Auschwitz – there was a terrible luxury. Rich Jews arrived with their belongings and were able to keep some. There was soap and perfume and fountain pens and watches. All amidst the chance of sudden and arbitrary death; amidst work-commandos from which the people returned so dead beat that, if they lived, they were sure to be picked out for the gas chamber at the next parade. All amidst the most horrible death, filth and squalor that could be imagined. The survivors of

Auschwitz were saved by being moved away to do work in towns like Hamburg and were then moved back to Belsen as we advanced.

At Auschwitz every woman had her hair shaved absolutely bald – many twice. I met pretty young girls whose hair was one inch long. They all had their numbers tattooed on their left arm. A mark of honour they will wear all their lives.

One of the most extraordinary things was the women and men (there are only a few men) who have kept themselves decent and clean. On the 5th day many girls had on powder and lipstick. The SS stores had been looted, and boots and clothes had been found.

Hundreds of people came up to me with letters which I have taken and am taking back to London to be posted all over the world. Many have lost all their relatives. 'My father and mother were burned' – 'My sister was burned'. This is what you hear all the time. The British Army is doing what it can. Units are voluntarily giving up blankets – 50,000 arrived whilst I was there and are being laundered. Sweet, chocolate and cigarette rations are being voluntarily given. Whilst I was there a long convoy of 240,000 hard rations arrived from Military Government – 4 days' reserve of biscuit, chocolate, tinned meats, etc.

The first day I recorded the Lasker sisters. They both helped French soldiers over the frontier. I also recorded Charlotte Gruno, a Berlin woman and a Dutchman. I met the Jewish Padre with the 2nd Army and we recorded the first eve of the Sabbath service in the camp. That evening I went back to the camp with Derek Sington, the political officer. He took me to the women's block at the end of the camp. We talked for a while to a group of Polish women. A group gathered: they wanted to know about Yalta and the Lublin* committee. They all wanted to go to Palestine.

We then talked with a pretty French woman of 24. She had been beaten by the Gestapo and had spent several years in concentration camps. She had done resistance work. Her hair an inch long. We talked in the open compound. In the middle was a pile of old

---

* The Polish Committee of National Liberation, also known as the Lublin committee, was an executive governing authority established by the Soviet-backed communists in Poland in the latter stages of the Second World War.

papers and skeletons. Around us were bodies of people who had died in the last 3 days. There were groaning and raving women lying around. And every few minutes, some woman groaning with typhus would stagger out and defecate there in the open. Where the French woman slept there were 10 healthy people and 50 sick and dying. She told us how she had seen corpses dragged off, under German command, by the still living, on ropes along the ground. Their heads were open where people had cut out the brains to eat. There had been cannibalism in the camp. The flesh, brains and livers of people who had died of typhus were eaten.

I gave this woman the good Luftwaffe watch I had been given at Brunswick.

21 April 1945

I went into the camp early. We recorded another Jewish service indoors. The Sabbath morning service. The people had made the Padre a little iced cake to welcome him. And as I came in they sang *Shalom Aleichem* (Welcome Unto You) – a rare honour for a Gentile. During the script and the reading of the traditional prayer for the dead, all around women and men burst into tears and cried openly. We were packed tight in a wooden hut, people standing to the walls. I then recorded a number of messages home in various languages.

Then we collected the orchestra together. They had got their instruments from the old camp band. Some of them played very well. They loved old jazz and played such tunes as 'I can't give you anything but love'. 'Alexander's Ragtime Band' they sang in English. One woman who played the violin burst into tears when we played the record back to her – 'I used to be able to play. I've played before big audiences. But I've forgotten how to play.'

Whilst we were walking in the camp one woman came up and begged for a cigarette. 'I'll give you bread for it' – and she showed me the loaf. Then we went to the children's hut. Before it is a pile of corpses there has been no time to move. We collected a choir of Russian girls from 12 to 14 and of Dutch boys and girls from 9 to 15.

They sang songs. The Russian children were very impressive – clean, quite big children. They had been looked after magnificently amidst starvation. They sang the songs they remembered from before captivity. They looked happy now. The Dutch children had been in the camp a long time and were very skinny and pale. We stood with our backs to the corpses out in the open amidst pines and birch trees, near the wire fence running round the camp.

I talked afterwards to a Dutch girl, Hetty Werkendamm, 15 years old, and her young brother. They had been 14 months in the camp. Their father and mother had worked in the workshops (where people were driven and beaten and died in hordes). Their mother had to get up at 3 to try and get some food for the husband to eat whilst he was at work. Their father had gone to work one day with a scarf around his neck. The SS men in charge had, out of sheer fun, taken hold of the ends of the scarf and half-strangled him. The little girl's stories went on endlessly: 'Once my father had to work,' she said, 'please excuse my language,' (she was a girl of 15) 'in the shit-pit. Right up to his arms, shovelling out the shit – saw him when he came back from work.'

Their mother and father had been taken away a month or so before. They were asking every officer they saw – 'How can we find out where our parents are?' The little girl said, 'If ever I meet those SS men again I'll kill them with my own hands. They made us stand on parade – children from 3 upwards – for hours on end in the snow.'

I also recorded an interview with a Russian girl, Olga Schlochberg, aged 14. Both her parents had been killed. She was a sturdy bright thing, who had learned some German.

late by now – about 8 and beginning to get dark. I went along to the cells where the SS men and women were kept. They were so worn out that they were being given a bit of a rest – so that more work could be got out of them – and they were now only 4 in a cell instead of 12. As we opened the cell door they all scrambled to attention – they had been got into a better frame of mind.

I called out one of them, a fair-haired weak-faced-looking man of 35. I talked to him in the corridor and there were guards with guns all around. They swore at the men and made them jump to it. I talked to the man very roughly, keeping him at attention. I told him he had very little chance of escaping execution as a war criminal. But he could help us and that might help him. I wanted a record describing what he had seen in the camps he had been in. I sent him back to the cell to think things over. I called out another: he turned out to be a Rumanian – I cursed him and sent him back. I then called out a doctor who looked in wicked shape. His head was bloody and his shirt torn and he looked as if one of his arms was broken. He had been at Auschwitz as a doctor. His story was that he had tended the inmates. In fact (I was told) he had conducted the experiments on women, deformed people and twins. He was no use to me: so I told him he hadn't long to live and sent him back.

I called out the first man again. He was ready to talk – he only asked that he could do it far enough away so that his comrades could not hear. We took him outside. And I recorded the interview. Then I went to the women's cell and got out at hazard the Overseer who had been in charge of the guards – a woman of 24. Obstinate and rather callous looking, with a hard brutal mouth. I kept her there standing at attention and started by telling her she was a war criminal, her uniform was a disgrace, and asked her questions. She had been at Auschwitz and put in charge of a camp. It was a model camp, she said – cinemas, etc. I laughed out loud. 'You expect us to believe that the SS spends money on Jews?' She kept on saying she was popular with the prisoners. 'If we let you out here away from these men you wouldn't live 2 minutes. Look at the guards we have to keep to protect you.' She admitted that she had helped to choose the women to be gassed at Auschwitz. 'You know that every prisoner here says that the SS women were even crueller than the men.'

'That's not true.'

'How many women have you beaten yourself? Did you have a whip?'

'I never had a whip in my hand.'

Well then, with the shining exception of yourself, who were so kind and so popular, how many women did the other SS women beat?'

'I don't want to lie. When women deserved it, I beat them – but only with my hand.' She said that many women in this camp would vouch for her kindness.

'Name any single prisoner in the camp you like, and I will have them sent for at once.'

No answer. She said she had many witnesses in another camp she had been in. I gave her pencil and paper and asked her to write down the names. She thought for a while and then said, 'It's no good. The whole camp will vouch for me.'

So I made her write down the name of the camp. 'You know you are a war criminal and war criminals will be tried and shot. You have a very slight chance of being alive long.'

'I have taken that into account. I don't count on being alive a year.'

Long silence.

'There is a way in which you might be able to help us. And if you help us, it might possibly help you.' And then I went on to say I wanted a record of her description of the camp.

There then ensued a long argument in which she tried to evade questions by asking me questions. At one time she said: 'If I don't do what you ask you'll shoot me. If I do it my own side will shoot me.'

'My God. Your side doesn't exist any more. Do you know how much of Germany we occupy? Leipzig, Regensburg, Frankfurt on Oder, suburbs of Berlin.'

I asked one of the soldiers for a newspaper. He produced a 4 days' old one and I showed her the map on the front page. She studied it a long time. It had a very marked effect on her. Then she began to plead to be allowed some time to consider.

'Five minutes.'

'Could I speak tomorrow morning? My voice is weak and hoarse. I'm so excited.'

'You must speak now or not at all. I can get some other woman to speak, and then I won't want you.'

'One favour. Can I have a cigarette?'

'If you do as I want you can have a cigarette.'

Then I sent one of the soldiers for a glass of water. And I let her sit down. She had been standing all this time – about half an hour.

She now mainly pleaded to be allowed till the morning. 'I'm still a human being.'

'Possibly.'

'I am a human being and I appeal to you as a human being. You are the stronger and we are the weaker. I am a woman.' Then she said she had heard we had concentration camps in England. I got very angry and told her how we had treated our Germans and our Fascists. Then she asked me what questions she would have to answer.

'Your name. Your age. Your service in the SS. Your description of things in this camp.'

'But that would incriminate all my colleagues here.'

'They are already fully incriminated. You can blame any higher SS people you like.'

'I don't want to mention any other names. Must I mention my own name?'

'Of course.'

Then she began to get hysterical. She drank water and looked at the cigarette I had put in front of her. She kept on putting her hands to her head and saying 'What am I to do?'

'I have been present at many interrogations and I know it won't do me any good whatever I do, either way.'

'It may do you good, I make no promises. But it's a matter of perfect indifference to me whether it's you or some other woman who speaks. A man has already spoken for me.'

'That I can believe.'

She was far pluckier than the man had been. She constantly looked me in the eyes. She sometimes set her mouth in an obstinate, cruel line. She probably expected to be beaten.

Then I suddenly became very firm. 'You must answer yes or no in one minute.' I set my stop watch going.

'Don't give me a time limit.'

'All right.' I stopped my watch. 'But I must have an answer quickly. If you don't answer I will take it as No. You will go back to your cell and I'll get someone else.'

She kept on putting her hands to her head and sipping water. 'You will only ask me the questions you have said?'

'Yes. Will you speak or not?'

A long silence. Then: 'Yes, if you only ask me those questions.'

So I got the mike and she went through her interview answering the questions in a low tense voice.

At the end I gave her a cigarette. Then she said: 'Now is the time for you to strike me.'

'We don't do that.'

'Can I smoke my cigarette here before I go back to my cell?'

'You may.' And I walked out.

That night when I got back about 11 very exhausted, I saw the Jewish Padre again and had a talk with him, as he was going to bed. Suddenly he broke down completely and sobbed out loud.

Reflections on Belsen

It is not enough to be horrified by Belsen, Buchenwald and the many other camps. It is important that we should feel horror, that we should be shocked into horrified belief. I think that is now happening in England. The things we have been told before and which we have only half-believed and then dismissed from our minds – these things have been told us now by photographs, by cinema, by recordings, by British soldiers.

We·believe them all right now. And we are appalled. But that is not enough. The intensity of the revulsion cannot last. Already, I find, people are beginning to ask questions. What is the explanation? What do these things mean for Europe? Did the German people know?

This last question can be answered. I spoke with a good many ordinary Germans around Belsen. I have spoken to soldiers and generals on this matter. I am convinced that very many Germans did not know about the exact details and the exact location of these camps. On these points they probably knew less than we did in the outside world. Belsen camp, for instance, was very strictly guarded. Anyone who came within 200 yards was shot. There was a big military camp next door and no one from it was allowed near Belsen, which was guarded exclusively by SS men and women.

But I am convinced that the Germans, though they did not know the exact details, knew in a general way about these camps. The same people who assure you they knew nothing – when you ask them 'Why didn't you do something against the Nazis?' –answer: 'It was impossible. The terror – the concentration camps.'

The guards in these camps mixed with the people and they must have told some stories; prisoners who were released told stories. The Gestapo itself allowed a generalised idea of the camps to get around. There was, I am quite sure, a generalised knowledge very widespread in Germany about concentration camps. Not exactly where they were – not exactly what happened in them. But knowledge that unspeakable things were being done on German soil.

The fact that the Nazis tried to hide the details and the fact that the German people had a very good general idea of what was afoot are both of extreme importance ...

Our army is doing a fine job in saving those who can still be saved. We are clearing the camps. Some will be burned and blotted from the face of the earth. Some, I hope, will be kept as memorials of shame forever.

We must do all we can to help the thousands of those men and women who have survived. But we must not do that and then turn our backs. For here we are face to face with evil. With an evil that seeks to destroy our civilisation at its roots. Here we face the real enemy with the mask off.

These camps like Belsen were not just a manifestation of sadism and persecution, of cruelty and oppression. Such things, though never remotely on this scale, have occurred in the history of all countries. They must be combatted and rooted out wherever they occur. But such occasional descents into cruelty have been departures from normally accepted standards – they have been condemned when discovered or defended by the perpetrators as sad necessities in special cases.

Not so camps like Belsen and Buchenwald.

Here there was deliberate, coldly calculated and coolly executed assault upon the very foundations of our Western life – which is the respect for individual human life, the distinction between the human and the animal.

In these camps the Nazis, with cold premeditation, treated human beings like animals. In Belsen they were in a planned way reduced to the level of animals deprived of the most elementary privacies, forced by hunger to fight one another for raw turnips – to sleep and live (and the children to play their pathetic occasional games) amongst corpses. In Auschwitz, women, twins and deformed people had experiments performed on them as if they were guinea pigs. People were deliberately picked out and slaughtered by the hundred thousand by gas and fire – as if they were noxious vermin.

These things were not done in the main by sadists – though the immediate instruments were often sadists. These things were not only done to persecute opponents – that at least is a rational end even if the means used by the Nazis were beyond civilised imagination. No: these things were done by men who knew what they were doing and why they were doing it.

They despise and hate our civilisation, our standards. They are not, I think, clear about what they want. But they are clear about what they want to destroy – respect for the individual human life. I am an historian. But I do not think in all history the world has ever been menaced by such naked evil, by evil so unabashed.

What are we to do about it?

We must remember first that this has happened in the midst of civilised Europe. And that it came very near success. It had the active support not only of Germans, but of many thousands of people in all countries. It had the tacit support of millions. Which of us has not shut our ears to these things? Which of us has not refused to believe them, or to believe them wholly?

The men of the Oxford Yeomanry whom I met at Belsen and who were the first British soldiers to enter that place of horror had a sure instinct. Over and over again they said: 'The only thing we are afraid of is that people will not believe at home. We didn't ourselves till we saw it.'

I think people at home believe now. Press, cinema and BBC have done their duty.

We must root these things out. The vengeance of the world must be relentless. There must be no mercy. But our vengeance must discriminate. If we wreak our wrath on guilty and innocent we shall undo our ends. Our aim must be to restore the respect for each individual human life – German lives too. And respect for human life means that there must be order, formality and proven guilt before any life is taken away.

We must not kill Germans indiscriminately. What then are we to do with them? They cannot escape a share of collective guilt and acquiescence. Not all of them. I have seen Germans – not Jews, but political prisoners, in Belsen. And in Nazi prisons. Germans have been amongst the victims.

We must remember, too, that the means of modem power are so enormous that a small number of men can exercise force over vast numbers. Even to the point, as we see today, of destroying their own country over their heads. That is what makes the menace of Belsen and Buchenwald so grave. The forces of evil have within their reach means never before known in history.

We can remember all this. But the problem remains – what are we to do about the Germans in whose midst these horrors have happened? I am not thinking about reparations. That problem is, morally at least, relatively simple. I am thinking of guilt, national guilt.

The only way back now – from the road that led to Belsen and Buchenwald – is that the German people admits and recognises, both openly and in its heart, that these 12 years have been the blackest in the whole of Europe's history. If this becomes part of the German conscience and tradition, there is some hope. If not, none.

If Germany looks back on Hitler as a great military leader and social innovator who nearly succeeded (as the French look on Napoleon) – if they look on Hitler as a lonely genius who was misinformed and badly served – even if they look upon him as a misguided adventurer who was nonetheless in the German tradition – then there can be no hope for Germany, or for a unified Western civilisation.

There is hope in the fact that the Nazis, despite their deliberate assault on Western culture, had to conceal the details of their camps from their own people. This means they knew they did not have the Germans with them in the most logical and open attacks of all they made upon the sanctity of human life. They had German support in much else: but not in this.

We must contribute to the purging of the German soul. In our country's policy, in our individual dealings with Germans, let us never forget the degradation, the crime against the West represented by Belsen and Buchenwald. There will be Germans who share our attitude. They have the main task of forming the national opinion of Germany.

German shame at Hitler's regime must appear, indelibly and beyond doubt, in German schools, in German history, in literature, in sermons, in cinemas, in conversation beyond chance of reversal.

Till then we will not be safe again.

Index